Organic Sweets and Treats

More Than 70 Delicious Recipes

An Imagine Book
Published by Charlesbridge
85 Main Street, Watertown, MA 02472
617-926-0329
www.charlesbridge.com

Created by Penn Publishing Ltd.
1 Yehuda Halevi Street, Tel Aviv, Israel 6513501
www.penn.co.il

Editor-in-Chief: Rachel Penn
Edited by Shoshana Brickman
Photography by Oded Marom
Design and layout by Ariane Rybski

© 2014 Charlesbridge Publishing

ISBN: 978-1-62354-039-5

2 4 6 8 10 9 7 5 3 1

For information about custom editions, special sales, premium and corporate purchases,
please contact Charlesbridge Publishing at specialsales@charlesbridge.com

Organic Sweets and Treats

More Than 70 Delicious Recipes

Michal Moses and Ivana Nitzan

PHOTOGRAPHY BY ODED MAROM

imagine!
Publishing

Contents

Sticks & Skewers

Cookies & Petits Fours

Cakes & Quick Breads

ABOUT THIS BOOK

The inspiration for this book comes from our reality in the modern world. We are mothers who want to treat our families to delicious sweets, but we don't want to compromise health. We are trying to find a balance between the pleasure of eating desserts with the importance of a diet rich in fruits, vegetables, nuts and whole grains. We also try to stay up-to-date with the latest health trends, and learn how to use raw materials that are as healthy and natural as possible. Of course, we also try to avoid processed foods as much as possible.

Food is an important pleasure of life, and enjoying what you eat (and what you serve to others) contributes to overall happiness. For that reason, we believe in eating healthy foods that are also delicious. Our priorities for the recipes in this book are good taste and pleasure, so while we certainly use healthy ingredients as often as possible, we never compromise taste in our efforts. In our approach, healthiness does not detract from flavor. These are healthy dishes you'll be thrilled to serve. We also believe appearance plays an important role in the enjoyment of eating. That's why we like to make our desserts look as lovely as possible. Not only is decorating desserts fun, but it also enhances people's enjoyment of them.

You may also notice that the serving sizes suggested in these recipes may be smaller than usual. This is because we truly believe that delicious treats can be just as satisfying in smaller portions. This means you can follow a healthier lifestyle without eliminating sweets—you just eat less of them. You'll find an example of this in the muffin recipes, where we recommend using cupcake pans because they are smaller than traditionally used muffin pans.

We warmly recommend (speaking from experience!) that you invite your children and spouses to join in the baking process. Not only does this increase their understanding of and respect for the effort that went into preparing these treats, but it also contributes to quality family time. Food brings people together; food preparation does this even more!

At the top of many recipes, you'll see these little icons:

Here's what they mean:

means the recipe is vegan. It contains no animal products.

means the recipe is dairy-free. It contains no dairy products.

means the recipe is gluten-free. It contains no products that have gluten.

We hope these icons help guide you when you are choosing recipes to prepare for yourselves and the people you love.

Ingredients

When we bake and cook, we try to use ingredients that are as healthy, natural and non-processed as possible. Thanks to the popularity of organic foods, these ingredients are quite easy to find. If you can't get them in your local supermarket or health food shop, you can certainly order them online.

AGAVE SYRUP comes from the agave cactus plant. It's thicker than water and thinner than honey, with a viscosity similar to that of maple syrup. Two versions of agave syrup are available: light syrup and dark syrup. The light version is less processed, has a bolder flavor and more minerals, too. The dark version is made at a lower temperature and is therefore suitable for people who only eat raw food.

Agave syrup is about one-and-a-half times as sweet as regular sugar and has a glycomic index 40% lower than ordinary sugar, so it is generally considered healthier. Also, because it comes from a plant, it is a vegan alternative to honey.

The ratio for replacing maple syrup or honey with agave syrup is 1:1. Using it to replace regular sugar is a bit more complicated since agave syrup does not have the same texture as sugar (it is a liquid and not a solid), therefore the way it reacts during baking is different. Because there is no straightforward formula for substituting agave syrup for white sugar, we tend to use white or brown organic cane sugar to replace white sugar.

ALMOND FLOUR is a gluten-free flour made from finely ground blanched almonds. It is sometimes used instead of wheat flour, though the resulting product won't rise as much as its wheat-based equivalent, and it will burn faster. Almond flour is difficult to make in a food processor at home, as the heat generated during the grinding process tends to produce an oily result (see Almond Meal, below). Foods made with almond flour rather than wheat flour have less carbohydrates and more calories.

ALMOND MEAL is what you get when you process whole blanched almonds in your food processor. It is oilier than almond flour, which is very hard to make with the tools most of us have in our kitchen.

CHIA SEEDS are rich in omega-3, antioxidants, fiber, phytonutrients, protein and energy.

COCOA BUTTER CHIPS are made from the fat extracted from cocoa beans during the chocolate-making process. Add melted cocoa butter chips to chocolate to make it easier to pour.

COCONUT OIL has recently gained international fame due to its high levels of omega-3 fatty acids. In sweet recipes, it adds a slightly nutty flavor, though it generally doesn't alter the flavoring in savory recipes. Coconut oil is solid at room temperature (this is particularly true if your kitchen tends to be cool) so you may need to melt it gently in the microwave or on the stove. Make sure that the ingredients you'll be mixing it with are slightly warm or at room temperature, so that the coconut oil stays in its liquid form.

DATE HONEY (Silan) is a natural sweetener, made entirely from pressed dates, is an excellent vegan alternative to honey.

DATE SPREAD is made entirely from dates, this sweet spread can be used instead of jam. It has a lovely soft texture and excellent flavor.

GOJI BERRIES are cultivated in China for generations and have recently made their way into kitchens in North America and Europe. They have a very high concentration of protein, antioxidants and trace minerals.

GRAPE SEED OIL is made from grape seeds. It has a neutral flavor and is rich in vitamin E and omega-6 polyunsaturated fat.

OAT FLOUR is made by processing old-fashioned rolled oats in a food processor or blender until they are finely ground. If you use gluten-free rolled oats, you'll have gluten-free flour.

ORGANIC CANE SUGAR comes in both white and brown varieties, and is made entirely from sugar cane, unlike regular sugar which is made from both beets and sugar cane, or only from beets. Cane sugar tastes better than ordinary sugar and produces better results in some recipes.

OLD-FASHIONED ROLLED OATS are a nutritious grain, packed with thiamine, vitamin E, iron and other nutrients. Oats are naturally gluten-free, but often have traces of gluten, so if you are avoiding gluten, make sure the oats you buy are labeled gluten-free. Oats can be used in their whole form to make granola and oatmeal, or processed into a flour (see Oat Flour on previous page) to make a wide variety of other treats.

QUINOA is a gluten-free pseudo cereal is rich in protein, minerals and fiber. It's nutty and delicious too! Most shops sell ivory quinoa, known simply as quinoa. Black quinoa grains are smaller than ivory quinoa grains. They have a crunchier texture, and the same great flavor and nutritional qualities.

SPELT FLOUR has a great nutritional profile and excellent flavor. It has a nutty, slightly sweet flavor that is similar to whole-wheat flour, but has more protein and is easier to digest.

TAHINI is a creamy, smooth and thick paste made from sesame seeds. Naturally rich in calcium and iron, it is a staple in the Mediterranean kitchen. Tahini can be thinned with water or lemon juice and is popular in both savory and sweet dishes. For best flavor and nutritional value, use organic tahini made from whole sesame seeds.

TAPIOCA is a gluten-free starch, which comes from the root of the cassava and is sold in both flour and whole pearl form. As flour, it can be used to thicken soups, stews and other cooked dishes. In pearl form, it is often served as a dessert. The pearl form comes in small and large sizes. Raw tapioca pearls are white and they become transparent as they are cooking, looking ultimately like jelly balls when fully cooked.

Though most of the recipes in this book use standard baking techniques, there are a few techniques that are not as well known. We hope you find the guidelines below helpful.

How to Cook Tapioca Pearls

Tapioca pearls are often used to make a thick Asian-style dessert pudding that is served chilled with lots of coconut milk and fresh fruit. Tapioca pearls can also be added to savory dishes and soups, creating a lovely appearance and texture.

In most cases, tapioca pearls should be boiled in water before they are added to a dish. Cook the pearls in plenty of water and stir them often to prevent them from sticking. Small tapioca pearls generally need to cook for about 25 minutes; larger ones require about 40 minutes of cooking time. Both types of pearls should be left to sit in the cooking water for another 15 minutes after it has been removed from the heat.

You'll know the tapioca is ready to eat when the pearls are completely transparent. Rinse the cooked tapioca pearls in warm water and then add them to the dish.

How to Make Cake Pops

Cake pops are a beautiful, trendy dessert that can be as gourmet-style as you like. They are fun to make, a pleasure to present, and delicious to eat. Although many cake pop recipes use processed frostings and sugary cake, cake pops can actually be made gourmet-style, using high quality and healthy ingredients. Here are some tips to get you started on making gourmet cake pops. For detailed recipes and instructions, see pages 88 to 90 and pages 96 to 97.

Type of cake: You can make cake pops using a wide variety of homemade cakes, including carrot, banana and ginger. You can actually use any type of cake you like, as long as it crumbles well.

Type of frosting: Standard cake pop recipes combine crumbled store-bought cake with store-bought frosting that's loaded with sugar and fat.

This method may be simple, but it's just as easy (and much healthier!) to mix the crumbled cake with low-fat cream cheese, naturally sweet date spread or organic natural almond butter.

Type of coating: As with the other elements of this delicious treat, you can cover cake balls with gourmet toppings that are as beautiful as they are delicious. Try a basic pâte à glacer made with a deliciously versatile organic cashew coating (page 90) or organic chocolate (page 97). Either one of these coatings can be enhanced with toppings, such as toasted coconut or nuts.

To make sure your cake pops turn out beautifully, follow these simple guidelines:

- Make the balls relatively small—no more than 2 inches in diameter—so that they don't fall off the sticks.

- Make sure the crumbled cake you use to make the balls isn't too fatty or moist. If it is, the fat will 'sweat' out of the cake through the covering. You'll know the crumbled cake mixture is right when you can roll it into balls without having the crumbs stick to your hands.

- Prepare a Styrofoam block into which the sticks that support the cake balls will be inserted. Elevating the cake balls in this manner allows the coating to dry evenly all around, rather than laying the cake balls on a tray so that one side is flattened. After the topping has hardened, the cake balls can be arranged on one side in a box.

- Dip the top of the sticks in the topping before inserting them into the cake balls. This ensures that the cake balls are stuck from the inside, too.

- Prepare a large space in the freezer in advance so that the cake pops can be placed standing up on their sticks.

- Freeze the cake balls between rolling and coating them, as this helps the coating sticking to the cake, both around the stick and on the outside.

- If you find that a single layer of coating isn't thick enough, let the first coating harden and then dip the cake balls into the coating a second time.

How to Temper Chocolate

This technique can be used to make a hard chocolate coating for fresh fruit or cake pops. All you need is high quality chocolate and a food thermometer.

1. Chop all of the chocolate into large chunks and then set aside about 20% of it. So, if you'd like to make 10 ounces of tempered chocolate, set aside 2 ounces.

2. Chop the rest of the chocolate and melt it in a double boiler or microwave until the temperature is 131°F.

3. Add the chocolate that you set aside in step 1 and stir until the temperature drops to about 87°F.

4. To test whether the chocolate is tempered, dip a plastic spatula in so that the spatula is covered with a thin layer of chocolate.

5. Let the spatula sit at room temperature (about 70°F) for 3 to 5 minutes. By this time, the chocolate should have a nice shiny surface. If the chocolate hardens too quickly, the melted chocolate wasn't warm enough and needs to be heated a bit more. If the chocolate hasn't hardened after 6 or 7 minutes, the chocolate is too warm and needs to be cooled a bit.

How to Make Pâte à Glacer

This technique can be used to make a hard chocolate coating without a food thermometer. All you need is high quality chocolate and oil, at a ratio of 10:1.

1. Chop the chocolate into small chunks and melt it in a double boiler or microwave.

2. Mix in the oil until the texture is smooth and suitable for dipping.

3. If you plan on using the pate a glacer for dipping, transfer it to a narrow cup that is slightly wider than the foods you want to dip into it.

Pantry Perfect

Homemade Almond Milk

Makes 3½ cups

Almond milk is dairy-free, tasty, healthy and suitable for anyone who can't drink ordinary milk. It's a convenient substitute for regular milk and can be served with cereal and used to make warm drinks and shakes.

When making almond milk, it's important to plan in advance because the almonds need to soak in water overnight before being ground. If you're pressed for time, you can speed up the soaking process by soaking the almonds in boiling water for about 1 hour.

The thickness of the milk can be controlled by the amount of water you add to the ground nuts. For a rich result that's somewhat similar to cream, add about 1½ cups of water; for something thinner, add up to 3 cups of water.

Homemade almond milk does not go through a pasteurization process, so it has a relatively short life. It can be safely stored in the refrigerator for about 2 to 4 days.

INGREDIENTS

1 cup raw organic almonds

1½ to 3 cups water, plus more for soaking

2 organic dates, pitted and chopped, or 2 teaspoons organic date honey, honey or agave syrup

DIRECTIONS

1. One night in advance: Place the almonds in a large bowl and cover with plenty of water. Let the almonds sit for at least 8 hours, and up to 2 days, in the refrigerator. If you are short on time, boil a pot of water and let the almonds soak in it for at least 1 hour.

2. After the almonds have soaked sufficiently, they will be quite soft. Using your fingers, peel the skin off each nut.

3. Transfer the peeled almonds to a blender. Add 1½ cups water and the dates. Start blending the mixture, pulsing at first in order to break the nuts. Once the nuts are broken, continue blending for 3 to 4 minutes until smooth. Add up to 1½ cups more water until the desired consistency is reached.

4. Place a cheesecloth on top of a fine mesh strainer and place the strainer on top of a large bowl. Pour the almond milk through the cheesecloth and strainer to remove any remaining almond chunks.

5. Transfer the milk to a glass jar and refrigerate until ready to use. May be stored in the refrigerator for up to 4 days.

Homemade Cashew Milk

Makes 3½ cups

As with Homemade Almond Milk (page 16), this milk can be made as thick or thin as you like, simply by adjusting the amount of water. The basic ratio of water to nuts is 4:1 (more than the ratio for the almond milk) and the soaking time is less.

INGREDIENTS

1 cup raw organic cashews

4 cups water, plus more for soaking

2 organic dates, pitted and chopped, or 2 teaspoons organic date honey, honey or agave syrup

DIRECTIONS

1. **At least 4 hours in advance:** Place the cashews in a large bowl and cover with plenty of water. Let the cashews sit overnight, or for at least 4 hours. If you are short on time, boil a pot of water and let the cashews soak in it for at least 1 hour. Drain the water.

2. Transfer the cashews to a blender, and add the dates and about half of the water. Start blending the mixture, pulsing at first, in order to break the nuts. Once the nuts are broken, continue blending for 3 to 4 minutes, gradually adding the water until the mixture is smooth and the desired consistency is reached.

3. Place cheesecloth on top of a fine mesh strainer and place the strainer on top of a large bowl. Pour the cashew milk through the cheesecloth and strainer to remove any remaining cashew chunks.

4. Transfer the milk to a glass jar and refrigerate until ready to use. May be stored in the refrigerator for up to 4 days.

Natural Yogurt

Makes 1 quart

Making your own natural yogurt is easier than you think. All you need is a carton of milk and some store-bought yogurt that contains live active cultures. This recipe includes exact temperatures, but you can make yogurt without measuring the temperature. Just make sure that you mix the fresh milk with the live active cultures and wait until the milk eventually becomes yogurt. The process occurs at room temperature in a relatively warm environment. Don't worry—the milk won't go bad. The process should be stopped when the milk takes on the desired sourness. Then all you need to do is transfer it to the refrigerator. Homemade yogurt is also a great way of controlling the fat content of the yogurt you eat, as it will be identical to that of the milk you choose to make it with.

INGREDIENTS

1 quart organic milk

3 tablespoons organic yogurt that contains live active cultures

1 tablespoon organic cane sugar

DIRECTIONS

1. In a small saucepan, heat the milk over medium heat until it starts to boil. If you are using a thermometer, it will reach a temperature of 180°F.

2. Remove the milk from the heat and let it cool to 115°F. If you don't have a thermometer, this is the temperature at which the milk is still warm, but you can put your finger in it without discomfort.

3. Pour a bit of the warm milk into a small cup and mix it with the live active cultures and the sugar. Pour this milk mixture back in with the rest of the milk and mix until combined.

4. Transfer the mixture to a sterilized jar, cover and let it rest in a warm place for several hours, and up to 1 day. The process usually takes about 8 hours, depending on the temperature of the room.

5. When the yogurt has reached the desired level of sourness (you'll only know this by tasting), transfer it to the refrigerator to chill thoroughly. You won't be able to check the yogurt's thickness at this stage because the thickening occurs as the yogurt chills. Chill the yogurt for several hours, overnight if possible, and serve chilled. May be refrigerated for up to 5 days.

Sweet Halva Spread

Makes 1½ cups

Halva is the peanut butter of children in the Mediterranean. It is based on tahini, a sesame seed paste that's rich in iron and calcium. Simply mixing it with date honey transforms it into a delicious sweet spread that's perfect for filling sandwiches.

INGREDIENTS

1 cup organic pure tahini

½ to ⅓ cup organic date honey, honey, maple syrup or agave syrup

DIRECTIONS

1. In a medium bowl, using a wire whisk, combine the tahini and date honey until a smooth paste forms. This could take a few minutes of whisking, so make sure you have energy.

2. Serve immediately or transfer to an airtight container and refrigerate for up to 2 weeks. Remove from the refrigerator about 15 minutes before serving so the mixture can soften a bit.

Classic Granola

Makes 7 cups

This classic blend of oats, seeds and dried fruit is delicious and nutritious. Serve with yogurt, milk or fresh fruit for a delicious snack, dessert or breakfast. If you are using pecans, add them near the end of the roasting period (during the last 10 minutes), as they are more delicate than other nuts and toast quickly. You can also use raw nuts, of course; raw nuts are healthier than roasted nuts, but have less flavor.

INGREDIENTS

4 cups organic gluten-free old-fashioned rolled oats

1½ cups mixed organic nuts (such as walnuts, pecans and cashews)

1¼ cups raw organic seeds (such as sunflower, pumpkin, flax and sesame)

6 tablespoons organic coconut oil or melted organic butter

½ cup organic cane sugar or organic brown cane sugar

¼ cup organic date honey, honey, maple syrup or agave syrup

⅛ teaspoon sea salt

¼ teaspoon organic ground cinnamon

1 cup chopped organic dried fruit mix (such as cranberries, dates, figs, cranberries and apricots)

DIRECTIONS

1. Preheat the oven to 350°F and line a baking sheet with parchment paper.

2. In a large bowl, combine the oats, nuts and seeds. If you are using pecans, don't add them yet.

3. In a small saucepan over medium heat, heat the oil, sugar, honey, salt and cinnamon until the sugar dissolves.

4. Pour the oil mixture into the oat mixture and stir until evenly coated.

5. Spread the granola evenly on the baking sheet and bake for about 15 minutes. Remove from the oven, mix again, and then return to the oven for another 20 minutes, baking until golden. If you are using pecans, add them during the last 10 minutes of baking.

6. Remove from the oven and set aside to cool; then crumble the cooled granola with your hands and mix in the dried fruit.

7. Transfer the granola to an airtight container and store in a dry place for up to 2 weeks.

Makes 4½ cups

Tahini is a wonderfully nutritious Mediterranean staple made from ground organic sesame seeds. Filled with calcium and iron, it is extremely versatile and integrates smoothly into both salty and sweet dishes.

INGREDIENTS

3 cups organic gluten-free old-fashioned rolled oats

1 cup raw organic nuts (such as pistachios and walnuts)

¼ cup organic sunflower seeds

¼ cup organic flax seeds

1 tablespoon organic chia seeds

¾ cup organic date honey, honey, maple syrup or agave syrup

½ cup organic pure tahini

1 cup chopped organic dried fruit mix (such as raisins, apricots and dates)

DIRECTIONS

1. Preheat the oven to 350°F and line a baking sheet with parchment paper.

2. In a large bowl, combine the oats, nuts and seeds.

3. In a small bowl, combine the date honey and tahini.

4. Add the honey mixture to the oat mixture and stir until evenly coated.

5. Spread the granola evenly on the baking sheet and bake for about for 15 minutes. Remove from the oven, mix again, and then return to the oven for another 20 minutes until golden.

6. Set aside to cool and then crumble with your hands and mix in the dried fruit.

7. Transfer the granola to an airtight container and store in a dry place for up to 2 weeks.

Coconut Chantilly

Makes 1 cup

This vegan whipped cream is made with coconut cream, which is essentially coconut milk with a higher percentage of fat. If you can't find anything in your supermarket called coconut cream, look for full-fat coconut milk. Coconut Chantilly is lighter than regular whipped cream, and you don't need to worry that it will turn into butter if you overwhip it. If the cream loses its volume, just chill it again and rewhip it.

Make sure you start preparing this recipe a night in advance by chilling the coconut cream. When making the cream, you'll only be whipping the part it that reduces when chilled (explained further below).

INGREDIENTS

One 13½-ounce can organic coconut cream

2 tablespoons organic cane confectioners' sugar

A few drops of organic pure vanilla extract or a few vanilla seeds

DIRECTIONS

1. **One night in advance:** Place the coconut cream in the refrigerator to chill.

2. **Same day:** Ten minutes before you plan to begin, place the mixing bowl in the freezer to chill thoroughly.

3. Remove the can of coconut cream from the refrigerator and turn it upside-down on your work surface. Open the cream from the base. You'll notice that the solids in the cream have settled here during the chilling process. Remove these solids and set them aside for another use. Transfer the rest of the cream (the part that is still in a liquid form) to the chilled mixing bowl.

4. Add the confectioners' sugar and vanilla, and whip until light and fluffy. Serve immediately or chill until ready to serve.

5. If the whipped cream starts to lose volume, you may re-chill and rewhip it.

Fresh Fig Jam

Makes 4 pints

This delicious jam is made without any added sugar or pectin. You'll use maple syrup for the sweetener, and apple peels and chia seeds rather than pectin to give the jam its signature gelatin-like texture. The chia seeds help eliminate any excess liquid. We've added rose water and cinnamon for extra flavor, but you can leave these spices out, or add lemon zest instead.

In ordinary jam, the added sugar helps preserve the fruit which means the jam doesn't need to be refrigerated. Because this jam has no sugar added, you'll need to store it in the refrigerator. Though it can last for up to two weeks in the refrigerator, it seldom lasts that long.

INGREDIENTS

8 cups stemmed and coarsely chopped fresh organic figs

1 to 1½ cups organic honey, date honey, maple syrup or agave syrup

2 tablespoons fresh organic lemon juice

Grated peel from 2 organic apples (also add the apple flesh if you like)

1 organic cinnamon stick

Organic pure vanilla extract or rose water

¼ cup organic chia seeds

DIRECTIONS

1. In a large heavy-bottomed pot, combine the figs, honey, lemon juice, grated apple peel and cinnamon stick. Bring to a boil over medium heat, stirring constantly. You may have to add a bit of water at the beginning of the cooking process so that the figs don't stick to the bottom of the pot.

2. When the mixture reaches a boil, reduce the heat to low and simmer, covered, for about 1½ hours, until you achieve the desired texture. Using a slotted spoon, remove any foam that forms while the jam is cooking.

3. When the mixture is ready, remove the cinnamon stick and apple peels, and mix in the vanilla extract and chia seeds. Let the jam cool for several hours.

4. Transfer the cooled jam to glass jars and store in the refrigerator for up to 2 weeks.

Makes 6 cups

Applesauce isn't just a tasty and nutritious snack on its own; it's also an excellent substitute for oil and eggs when you bake. If you want to reduce the amount of oil in a recipe, simply replace some of it with applesauce. You can often replace 1 large egg with 2 ounces of applesauce, though this conversion won't work in recipes in which the eggs provide volume, such as soufflés and sponge cakes.

When you make applesauce, make sure you choose sweet apple varieties, such as Fuji, Red Delicious, Yellow Delicious or Royal Gala. Sour varieties such as Granny Smith will produce a sour applesauce that requires additional sweetening. For a truly rich flavor, we suggest using a combination of apple types. If all the varieties are sweet, you won't need to add any sweetener.

When cooking the apples, they should be cored but not peeled, since the peel adds nutrition and texture, thanks to its natural pectin. Don't worry about having pieces of peel in your applesauce, since these will be removed when you pour the applesauce through a strainer.

The juices from the apples aren't released at the very beginning of the cooking process, so you'll have to add a bit of liquid, either water or pure apple juice, right at the start so that the apples don't get scorched. As the apples cook, you could add ground cinnamon or cloves for extra flavor. If you plan on using the applesauce as a replacement for butter or oil, leave it plain so that it is as versatile as possible.

This recipe can be easily adapted to include as many apples as you like. Just make sure you have a significant quantity to start (at least 4 pounds) so that there is enough apple to absorb all the water added to prevent scorching.

INGREDIENTS

4 pounds sweet organic apples (such as Fuji, Red and Yellow Delicious and Royal Gala)

Water or organic pure apple juice

Freshly squeezed organic lemon juice

DIRECTIONS

1. Core the apples and cut them into even slices. The thinner the slices, the quicker the apples will cook. Try to keep all the slices more or less the same size so that they cook at the same rate. Place the apples in a heavy-bottomed pot with a lid.

2. Add enough water or apple juice to cover the bottom of the pan, plus a few drops of lemon juice. Cover and bring to a gentle boil over medium heat.

3. Reduce the heat to low and continue cooking very gently for about 30 minutes, until the apples are completely soft. Check the contents of the pan occasionally to make sure the apples aren't sticking to the bottom. If the apples don't release enough juice, they will stick, so add a few more drops of water or juice to prevent this from happening.

4. If some apples have scalded at the bottom, transfer the rest of the apples to a different pan and continue cooking. Don't scrape off the apples that are stuck on the bottom, as this will ruin the flavor of the applesauce.

5. If the apples release too much liquid as they cook, remove the cover of the pan and let the liquid steam off.

6. When the apples are soft, remove from the heat and allow them to cool slightly, then transfer to a food processor and blend until smooth. If you like your applesauce chunky, blend it a bit less. Pour the applesauce through a fine mesh strainer to remove any peels, and then set aside to cool.

7. Transfer the cooled applesauce to airtight containers and store in the refrigerator for up to 5 days. May be frozen for up to 2 months.

Chocolate Ganâche

Makes 2½ cups

Everyone needs a go-to recipe for topping baked treats and this is one of our favorites. It does require a bit of planning, as the mixture needs to be refrigerated overnight, but the result is worth it! With just two ingredients, you'll be able to make a rich and delicious frosting that's perfect for topping all sorts of cakes and cupcakes.

INGREDIENTS

9 ounces organic dark chocolate, coarsely chopped

One 13½-ounce can organic coconut cream

DIRECTIONS

1. Place the chocolate in a heatproof bowl. In a small pot, heat the coconut cream until it almost boils.

2. Pour the coconut cream onto the chocolate and mix until smooth. Let the mixture cool to room temperature and then transfer to the refrigerator and chill overnight.

3. May be stored in the refrigerator for up to 2 weeks.

4. Just before serving, transfer the chilled chocolate mixture to a large mixing bowl and whip until light and airy.

Delish in a Dish

Chocolate Avocado Mousse (page 38)

Makes 10 pancakes

To make these pancakes both gluten-free and dairy-free, replace the butter with oil and replace the buttermilk with almond milk or coconut milk. You can add vanilla, cinnamon or nutmeg to the batter, though leaving the pancakes without flavorings means they can be served with a greater variety of toppings.

INGREDIENTS

2 large ripe organic bananas, mashed

1 tablespoon melted organic butter, canola oil or coconut oil

½ teaspoon organic lemon juice

1 tablespoon organic maple syrup, plus more for serving

¼ cup organic buttermilk, almond milk or coconut milk

2 large organic free-range eggs, room temperature

¾ cup gluten-free organic oat flour

¼ cup organic brown rice flour

½ teaspoon baking soda

½ teaspoon salt

Canola oil, for frying

Coconut Chantilly (page 23), for serving

1 large ripe organic banana, sliced, for serving

Organic maple syrup, for serving

DIRECTIONS

1. In a large bowl, combine the bananas, butter, lemon juice and maple syrup. Mix until a paste forms.

2. Mix in the buttermilk and eggs until evenly combined.

3. In a separate bowl, combine the oat flour, rice flour, baking soda and salt. Make a hole in the middle of the dry mixture and pour in the wet mixture.

4. Stir just until the ingredients combine, making sure not to overmix. Set the mixture aside for 10 minutes.

5. Heat a large nonstick frying pan over medium heat and brush with a thin coating of oil. Pour 2 or 3 tablespoons of batter onto the pan in three different places, leaving space between each pancake so that they do not stick together.

6. Cook until bubbles appear on the surface of the pancake, and then use a long thin spatula to flip each pancake. Cook on the other side for another minute or two.

7. When the pancakes are golden on both sides, transfer to a large plate. Repeat with the remaining batter. Serve warm, topped with Coconut Chantilly, banana slices and maple syrup.

Makes 5 servings

This dairy-free treat is made with coconut milk and lots of fresh fruit. The tapioca pearls are cooked in advance (page 11) and then left to chill, overnight if possible, with the coconut milk. Prepare the mango puree and fruit topping just before serving for a delicious combination of flavors and color.

INGREDIENTS

4½ cups water

½ cup organic tapioca pearls

½ cup organic cane sugar or agave syrup

⅔ cup organic coconut milk

3 organic mangoes, peeled, pitted and cut into chunks

¼ organic pineapple, peeled, cored and cut into chunks

1 large organic banana, sliced

Organic shredded coconut, for topping

DIRECTIONS

1. In a large pot, bring the water to a boil over medium-high heat. Add the tapioca pearls, reduce the heat to medium and cook, stirring occasionally until completely transparent. For small tapioca pearls, cooking time will be about 25 minutes; for larger pearls, it will take about 40 minutes. When the pearls are almost transparent, mix in the sugar.

2. Remove the tapioca from the heat and drain; then wash under cool running water to remove excess starch and prevent the pearls from sticking.

3. Transfer the tapioca to a large bowl and pour in the coconut milk. Cover and refrigerate until thoroughly chilled, preferably overnight.

4. Just before serving, transfer the fruit of two of the mangoes to a food processor and process until smooth. Distribute the mango puree evenly among the serving glasses and top with the chilled tapioca pudding.

5. Distribute the mango chunks of the remaining mango, along with the pineapple chunks and banana slices, evenly among the glasses. Top with dried coconut and serve.

Makes 5 servings

INGREDIENTS

Fruit Compote

4 cups water

2 tea bags, green tea or fruit infusion

2 organic dried apricots, cut lengthwise, or 2 organic dried figs, coarsely chopped

¼ cup organic raisins or organic dried blueberries

2 teaspoons crushed fresh organic ginger

10 organic cardamom pods

½ bunch fresh organic mint

2 pounds fresh organic summer fruit (such as peaches, nectarines, plums, blueberries, raspberries, cherries and grapes), pitted and chopped

A few drops of agave syrup or maple syrup

Blackberry liqueur (such as Crème de Cassis), dessert wine or dry white wine, optional

Tapioca

8 cups water

1 cup large tapioca pearls

This light and refreshing appetizer is egg-free, gluten-free, and filled with preserved summer fruit. Start with spiced cooking liquid, add dried fruit to sweeten, and then add fresh fruit during the last few moments of cooking. Compote can be served warm or chilled. If you're making it with fresh summer fruit in season, we recommend serving it chilled, with plain organic yogurt.

Letting the compote steep for about 30 minutes allows it to gain sweetness and flavor. If it's still not sweet enough after 30 minutes, add a bit of agave syrup.

Although tapioca pearls don't add any taste, we do like to add them for texture. When adding tapioca, cook the pearls separately and then add them just before serving. See page 11 for details on how to cook tapioca pearls.

DIRECTIONS

1. **Prepare the compote:** Pour the water into a large pot and then add the tea bags, dried fruit, ginger and cardamom; set aside a few mint leaves and add the mint as well. Bring to a boil over medium heat and then cook for about 10 minutes.

2. Remove the mixture from the heat and let it cool until tepid. Pour the mixture through a fine mesh strainer to remove the tea bags, cardamom and mint leaves, and return the liquid to the pot.

3. Mix in the fruit and bring the mixture to a boil; then reduce the heat to a gentle boil and cook for about 15 minutes. Test for sweetness; if the compote isn't sweet enough, add a bit of agave syrup. Set aside to cool and then refrigerate until chilled.

4. **While the compote is chilling, prepare the tapioca pearls:** Pour 8 cups of water into a large pot and bring to a boil. Add the tapioca pearls, mixing gently to make sure that they don't stick to each other.

(continued on page 38)

(continued from page 36)

Cook for about 40 minutes, until the tapioca pearls float on the top of the water and are completely transparent.

5. Drain the tapioca pearls and wash under cold water to stop the cooking process. Transfer to an airtight container, add a bit of water, and refrigerate until ready to serve.

6. Just before serving, mix in the chilled tapioca pearls, remaining mint leaves, and the crème de cassis.

Chocolate Avocado Mousse

Makes 4 servings

See photo page 30

Here's an elegant vegan dessert that's sure to impress. Instead of coconut cream, you can use homemade cashew or almond milk that is relatively thick. The dates can be replaced with maple syrup, agave syrup or honey. If you like your mousse sweet, add an extra date or two.

INGREDIENTS

4 ripe organic avocados

½ cup organic coconut cream

½ cup organic cocoa powder

4 soft organic dates, pitted and peeled

½ cup brandy or cherry liqueur, optional

DIRECTIONS

1. Cut the avocados in half and remove the flesh using a large spoon. Transfer the avocado flesh to a food processor or mixing bowl.

2. Add the coconut cream, cocoa powder, dates and brandy. Process or mix until smooth.

3. Transfer to the refrigerator and chill for at least 2 hours. Serve chilled.

4. May be refrigerated in an airtight container for up to 1 day.

Organic Sweets and Treats

Banana Date Ice Cream

Makes 1½ cups

This naturally sweet dessert is a delicious no-bake way of using bananas that are just a bit too ripe. Sweet and satisfying it has just the right combination of smooth bananas and crunchy nuts.

INGREDIENTS

4 large ripe organic bananas, peeled, cut into thirds and frozen

5 large organic dates, pitted

1 to 2 tablespoons organic coconut cream

2 tablespoons chopped organic walnuts

DIRECTIONS

1. Place the bananas and dates in a food processor and process until smooth.

2. Gradually add the coconut cream until you achieve just the right thickness. Mix in the walnuts until evenly combined.

3. Serve immediately or freeze until ready to serve.

4. May be frozen in an airtight container for up to 2 weeks.

Oat & Berry Porridge

Makes 4 servings

The essence of comfort food, this dish is made with a combination of Homemade Cashew Milk (page 17) and water. You can also make it with almond milk, walnut milk or dairy milk. For an extra boost of nutrition, goji berries make an excellent and flavorful addition.

INGREDIENTS

3 cups water

Pinch of salt

2 cups organic gluten-free old-fashioned rolled oats

¼ cup organic maple syrup, agave syrup, date honey or honey

1 cup organic cashew milk, almond milk or dairy milk

1 teaspoon organic pure vanilla extract

1 cup fresh organic raspberries, for serving

½ cup raw organic nuts (such as almonds and walnuts), for serving

DIRECTIONS

1. In a small pot, bring the water to a boil. Add the salt.

2. Mix in the oats and maple syrup, and cook at a gentle boil for about 10 minutes, stirring constantly. As the oatmeal thickens towards the end of the cooking period, slowly mix in the milk and vanilla extract. Cook until the oatmeal is soft.

3. Serve warm, topped with fresh raspberries and mixed nuts.

Grilled Fruit with Mascarpone Cream

Makes 6 servings

This recipe works best with relatively stable fruit, such as pineapples and peaches, which don't fall apart when they are grilled. Brush the fruit with bit of coconut oil and grill until the natural sugars in the fruit caramelize and grill signs are visible. No need to add sweetener because nature has given them just the right amount of sweetness—trust us.

You can make this dish with the mascarpone cheese topping described below or serve with Coconut Chantilly (page 23). For an even simpler alternative, serve with flavored yogurt, soft goat cheese or mascarpone cheese flavored with honey and vanilla. For a sweet and sour touch, ` drizzle balsamic vinegar syrup on the grilled fruit.

INGREDIENTS

1 organic mango, peeled, pitted and sliced

½ organic pineapple, sliced in rounds

1 organic peach, pitted and sliced

Organic coconut oil or canola oil, for brushing

8 ounces mascarpone cheese

2 tablespoons organic brown cane sugar

½ vanilla pod or ½ teaspoon organic pure vanilla extract

Grated zest from 1 organic lemon

Organic mint leaves, for garnish

Toasted organic almond slivers, for garnish

DIRECTIONS

1. Preheat the oven to 400°F. Brush the mango, pineapple and peach slices with coconut oil and broil until grill marks appear.

2. In a small bowl, combine the cheese, sugar, vanilla and lemon zest. Mix until combined and then chill until ready to serve.

3. Served the chilled fruit with the mascarpone cream. Garnish with fresh mint leaves and toasted almond slivers.

Black Quinoa Breakfast

Makes 4 servings

This comforting dish makes a satisfying breakfast (or supper). Healthier and more interesting than ordinary porridge, black quinoa is gluten-free, rich in protein and minerals, and easy to digest. Serve with organic fresh and dried fruit, raw seeds and nuts.

INGREDIENTS

1 cup organic black quinoa

2 cups organic almond milk, cashew milk or dairy milk, plus more for serving

¼ teaspoon organic pumpkin pie spice or another seasoning

Grated zest from 1 organic orange, optional

Pinch of sea salt

2 to 3 tablespoons organic honey, date honey, maple syrup or agave syrup

Organic fresh fruit, dried fruit, mixed nuts or seeds, for serving

DIRECTIONS

1. Rinse the quinoa under running water and drain thoroughly.

2. In a small pot, bring 2 cups of milk to a boil over medium-high heat. Mix in the quinoa, pumpkin pie spice, orange zest and sea salt, and bring the mixture to a boil again. Then cover, reduce the heat to low, and cook gently for about 20 minutes.

3. Add the honey and cook for another 5 minutes, until the quinoa is soft.

4. Remove from the heat and let it sit for about 10 minutes to allow the excess liquid to evaporate.

5. Serve warm, with milk, fresh fruit, dried fruit, nuts and seeds.

Rye Buttermilk Pancakes

Makes 4 servings

If you like, enrich the batter with coconut or chunks of date. You can also serve with a heaped serving of fresh fruit salad.

INGREDIENTS

½ cup organic whole-wheat flour

½ cup organic rye flour

2 teaspoons organic baking powder

¼ teaspoon organic ground cinnamon

1 tablespoon organic cane sugar

¼ teaspoon salt

2 large ripe organic bananas, mashed

1 cup organic buttermilk, almond milk or coconut milk

1 large organic free-range egg, room temperature

Canola oil, for frying

Organic maple syrup, honey or date honey, for serving

DIRECTIONS

1. In a large bowl, combine the flours, baking powder, cinnamon, sugar and salt.

2. In a separate bowl, combine the bananas, buttermilk and egg.

3. Make a hole in the middle of the dry mixture and pour in the banana mixture. Stir just until the ingredients combine and make sure not to overmix. Set the mixture aside for 10 minutes.

4. Heat a large nonstick frying pan over medium heat and brush with a thin coating of oil. Pour 2 or 3 tablespoons of batter onto the pan in three different places, leaving space between each pancake so that they do not stick together.

5. Cook until bubbles appear on the surface of the pancake, and then use a long thin spatula to flip each pancake. Cook on the other side for another minute or two.

6. When the pancakes are golden on both sides, transfer to a large plate. Repeat with the remaining batter. Serve warm, topped with syrup.

Raspberry Morning Shake

Makes 2 to 4 servings

This drink is refreshing, nutritious and delicious. Excellent for a weekend breakfast, you can make it dairy-free by eliminating the goat yogurt and doubling the almond milk.

INGREDIENTS

¾ cup fresh or frozen organic raspberries

½ cup organic goat yogurt

Grated zest from ½ organic lemon

1 teaspoon organic pure vanilla extract or ground cardamom

2 tablespoons organic goji berries

1 tablespoon agave syrup

2 tablespoons organic chia seeds

1 tablespoon organic macadamia nuts

3 organic lettuce leaves

1 cup ice cubes

½ cup organic almond milk, cashew milk or rice milk

DIRECTIONS

1. Place the raspberries, yogurt, lemon zest, vanilla extract, goji berries, agave syrup, chia seeds, macadamia nuts, lettuce leaves, ice cubes and ¼ cup of the milk in a blender, and process until smooth.

2. Gradually add the remaining ¼ cup of milk until you reach the desired consistency. Serve immediately.

Buckwheat Crêpes

Makes 20 crêpes

This classic French crêpe can be used for both savory and sweet dishes. Buckwheat flour doesn't have any gluten, but we do recommend enriching the flavor with a bit of spelt flour (which does contain gluten). For best results, prepare the batter one day in advance and let it sit in the refrigerator overnight. It's important to mix it every now and then, as buckwheat flour has a tendency to settle on the bottom.

Crêpes are a very convenient dish that can be made in advance and frozen for up to 2 months. First let the crêpes cool completely and then wrap them securely in plastic wrap before freezing. Let frozen crêpes thaw at room temperature for about 20 minutes and then heat them gently in a pan or microwave before serving.

INGREDIENTS

2 cups organic cashew milk, almond milk or dairy milk

3 large organic free-range eggs, room temperature

1 teaspoon organic cane sugar

¼ teaspoon salt

¾ cup organic buckwheat flour

½ cup organic spelt or whole-wheat flour

Canola oil, for frying

Fresh organic strawberries, for serving

Organic maple syrup, for serving

DIRECTIONS

1. In a large mixing bowl, combine the milk, eggs, sugar, salt and both flours. Mix until smooth. Transfer to an airtight container and refrigerate overnight. Make sure you stir the mixture every now and again to prevent the buckwheat flour from settling.

2. Remove the batter from the refrigerator and mix well. Heat a non-stick skillet over medium high heat and brush lightly with oil.

3. Pour in about ¼ cup of the batter and gently tilt the skillet to coat it evenly with batter. Cook for about 1 minute, until the top of the crêpe appears to have set, the bottom has brown spots, and the center is lifted by pockets of air.

4. Run a spatula around the edge of the crêpe to loosen it and then gently flip to the other side. Cook the other side for about 45 seconds, until small brown spots appear on this side too.

5. Repeat, cooking the crêpes one at a time, and stack on a large plate until they are all ready. Serve immediately with fresh strawberries and maple syrup.

Roasted Figs & Ricotta

Makes 4 servings

Roasted figs are delicious, impressive and so easy to prepare. As an alternative to the sweet topping described below, you could try a sweet-and-sour combination of honey and balsamic vinegar. The cheese adds just the right amount of saltiness and the rosemary imbues it all with a wonderful aroma.

If you like, replace the ricotta with gorgonzola, mascarpone or Saint Maure goat cheese. The pine nuts can be replaced with another type of nut, and you can use thyme instead of rosemary. With this incredibly versatile recipe, every addition or change you make leads to an entirely different result.

INGREDIENTS

8 fresh organic figs

2 teaspoons organic butter, olive oil or coconut oil

2 teaspoons organic honey, date honey, maple syrup or agave syrup

A few sprigs of rosemary, finely chopped

2 teaspoons masala wine or port, optional

1½ to 2 ounces ricotta cheese, crumbled

3 tablespoons organic pine nuts

DIRECTIONS

1. Preheat the oven to 400°F and line a baking sheet with parchment paper.

2. Using a small sharp knife, cut a deep double-X on the top of each fig, making sure not to cut all the way to the bottom. Gently press in the figs at the base to open the top for stuffing.

3. Place a bit of butter in the middle of each fig and then add the honey, rosemary, wine, ricotta and pine nuts.

4. Arrange the figs on the baking sheet and bake for about 15 minutes, until the figs are soft and golden, and the juices are released in a thick syrup. Serve warm.

Summer Fruit Crumble with Almonds & Oats

Makes one 2½-quart crumble

When summer fruits are too ripe to eat fresh, it's time to bake a crumble. You don't have to add much sweetener (a spoon or two of agave syrup is usually enough). Serve with natural yoghurt to highlight the flavor of the fruit and balance the sweetness.

When preparing the crumble, make sure the dough is cold and the layer of fruit isn't too hot. Otherwise, the crumble topping may melt when it comes in contact with the fruit before it has a chance to bake properly and turn crumbly. If you like to spice things up, add vanilla, cinnamon and ginger to the fruit medley.

INGREDIENTS

2 cups organic gluten-free old-fashioned rolled oats

3½ ounces organic butter, cold and cut into small cubes

⅔ cup organic almond flour

½ cup organic cane sugar

1¾ ounces raw organic nuts (almonds, walnuts or pecans), chopped

Organic butter or oil, for greasing

5 to 6 cups diced organic fresh summer fruit (such as plums, peaches, nectarines, figs, grapes, blueberries and raspberries)

1 or 2 tablespoons organic honey, date honey, maple syrup or agave syrup

DIRECTIONS

1. In a blender, process 1 cup of the oats into a fine meal. Transfer these oats to the bowl of an electric mixer and add the remaining cup of oats, as well as the butter, almond flour and sugar. Mix on medium speed until crumbly. Mix in the almonds until combined, and then transfer to an airtight container and refrigerate or freeze until ready to use.

2. Preheat oven to 330°F and grease a 2½-quart baking dish.

3. Place the fruit in a large bowl and mix in up to 2 tablespoons of honey until combined. Transfer the fruit mixture to the baking dish and pat into an even layer. Bake for 10 to 14 minutes, until the fruit is grilled, soft and golden and the juices have been released. Remove from the oven and cool to room temperature.

4. Transfer the cold crumble topping to the cooled fruit base and return to the oven. Bake for about 35 minutes, until the top is golden and the fruit is bubbling. Serve warm.

5. May be refrigerated in an airtight container for up to 3 days. Reheat gently before serving.

Chocolate Hazelnut Fondue

Makes 3 to 4 servings

Planning a small dinner party with friends? Here's a perfect way to close the meal and open the conversation. Make sure you have plenty of fresh fruit and enough long-necked forks for serving.

INGREDIENTS

3 tablespoons organic cocoa butter or coconut oil

3 tablespoons organic hazelnut butter or almond butter

5 tablespoons organic cocoa powder

2 to 3 tablespoons organic honey, date honey or agave syrup

Grated zest from 1 organic orange, optional

Up to ¼ cup water

1 to 2 teaspoons chocolate or orange liqueur, coffee or brandy

Fresh organic strawberries, pineapples, kiwis and other fruit, peeled and chopped

DIRECTIONS

1. Using a microwave or double boiler, melt the cocoa butter. Mix in the hazelnut butter, cocoa powder, honey and orange zest.

2. Gradually add the water, while mixing, until the mixture is smooth and thick, and then mix in the liqueur.

3. Transfer the hazelnut fondue to a serving bowl and serve immediately with fresh fruit.

4. Leftover fondue may be refrigerated in an airtight container for up to 4 days. Reheat gently to serve.

Poached Pears in Coconut Milk

Makes 4 servings

This elegant dessert is perfect for warming up when the weather gets cold. It's free of gluten, dairy and eggs. For a more indulgent dessert, replace half (or all!) of the coconut milk with coconut cream. Another way to thicken the sauce is to add a bit of tapioca flour to the liquid while it cooks. When you're cooking the pears, make sure that the coconut milk (or cream) is heated until just before it boils to make sure that the milk doesn't separate. Adding ginger gives the dish a bit of zing, but omit if you find this flavor too strong.

INGREDIENTS

One 13½-ounce can organic coconut milk

¼ cup maple syrup or agave syrup

4 ripe organic pears, peeled, halved and cored

½ teaspoon crushed fresh organic ginger, optional

4 ounces organic dark chocolate, coarsely chopped, for serving

2 tablespoons chopped toasted hazelnuts, for serving

DIRECTIONS

1. In a small saucepan, heat the coconut milk and maple syrup over medium-high heat until just before boiling point.

2. Add the pears and the ginger, reduce the heat to low and cook for about 25 minutes, until the pears are tender but still firm. Turn the pears carefully while they cook to make sure they cook evenly.

3. When the pears are almost ready, melt the chocolate using a double boiler or microwave.

4. Transfer the warm pears to individual serving dishes and drizzle with the cooking liquid. Drizzle melted chocolate over the top, sprinkle with nuts and serve.

5. May be stored in an airtight container for up to 2 days.

Spicy Rice Pudding

Makes 3 to 4 servings

Rice pudding is the ultimate comfort food, and surprisingly easy to make from scratch. You can use round white rice for a mushy, risotto-like texture although we prefer using long-grain rice, as it results in a delicate texture with distinct grains. You can top your pudding with fresh fruit as we've done here, or opt for a more aromatic topping of toasted nuts and cinnamon.

Rice pudding can be served warm or chilled. It can be served straight from the stovetop (pictured here), or thickened with egg yolks and baked (instructions below). Rice pudding can be stored for up to 3 days in the refrigerator.

INGREDIENTS

1 cup organic long-grain rice

2¼ cups water

½ teaspoon sea salt

¾ cup organic almond milk, cashew milk or dairy milk

½ cup organic coconut cream or dairy cream

¼ cup organic cane sugar or 3 tablespoons organic honey, date syrup or agave syrup

1 tablespoon organic light raisins, soaked in advance until soft

4 cardamom pods

1 organic cinnamon stick or ¼ teaspoon organic ground cinnamon

Organic coconut oil or butter, for greasing, optional

2 large organic free-range egg yolks, optional

1 organic mango, sliced, for serving

DIRECTIONS

1. Rinse the rice thoroughly under running water and then drain. Transfer to a medium pot, add the water and salt, and bring to a boil over medium-high heat. Cover the pot, reduce the heat to low, and cook for 30 to 40 minutes until the rice is soft and the water has evaporated completely. Remove the rice from the heat and let it sit for at least 10 minutes.

2. In a small pot, combine the milk, cream, sugar, raisins, cardamom and cinnamon, and bring to a boil over medium-high heat. Mix in the rice, reduce the heat to low, and cook for about 10 minutes, stirring constantly, until the liquid thickens slightly. Remove the mixture from the heat and let it cool until just warm. Remove the cardamom pods and cinnamon stick.

3. **To serve the pudding directly from the stovetop:** Distribute the pudding among four serving dishes, top with fresh mango slices and serve.

4. **To make a thicker pudding:** Preheat the oven to 180°F and grease four heat-resistant ramekins with coconut oil or butter. Line a baking tray with parchment paper.

5. Mix the egg yolks into the rice mixture and then distribute it evenly between the four ramekins. Arrange them on the baking tray and bake for about 20 minutes, until the tops are golden. The pudding will probably bubble as it bakes, so lining the baking tray saves cleanup later.

6. Remove the pudding from the oven and set aside to cool slightly and stabilize. Top with fresh mango slices and serve.

Makes 4 servings

This recipe is more of a method than a recipe. It's elegant, easy to prepare and features an irresistible combination of savory and sweet flavors. Just choose your favorite fruit and your favorite semi-stable cheese, and you're ready to go.

INGREDIENTS

4 cups fresh organic summer fruit (such as peaches, nectarines, plums, figs, berries and raspberries)

2 to 3 tablespoons organic coconut oil, canola oil, grape seed oil or light olive oil

2 tablespoons organic honey, date honey, maple syrup or agave syrup

¼ cup raw organic Brazil nuts or pecans

3½ ounces semi-stable cheese (such as Saint Maure, ricotta and gorgonzola), sliced

Organic mint leaves, for garnish

DIRECTIONS

1. Preheat the oven to 350°F and line a baking sheet with parchment paper.

2. Slice the fruit into thick slices and remove the pits, if required. Transfer to a medium bowl.

3. Drizzle with oil and honey, and then arrange in a single layer on the baking sheet. Sprinkle the nuts on top.

4. Bake for about 20 minutes, until the fruit is golden and soft and the juices are released.

5. During the last few minutes of cooking, add the cheese. Continue baking until the cheese is warm and just slightly melted. Garnish with fresh mint and serve warm.

Fruity Rainbow Shots

Makes 5 servings

This gorgeous drink combines great taste, bold flavors and a beautiful appearance. It's really easy to make too, since nature does most of the work. All you do is puree fresh fruit and stack it in a shot glass. If you like, enhance the flavor of the fruit purees with grated lemon zest, fresh ginger, vanilla extract, liqueur, or ground mint leaves. If the fruit is too sour, add a drop or two of agave syrup or honey to sweeten.

We recommend preparing this recipe just before you serve it in order to preserve as many of the vitamins as you can. In any case, it only takes a few minutes to prepare. It's also important to use chilled fruit, or add a little bit of ice to each puree, so that the result is refreshingly cold. You could also add a bit of yogurt, milk or cream to one of the layers to make it richer and a bit like a fresh fruit smoothie.

INGREDIENTS

½ cup chilled fresh organic raspberries (or frozen and thawed)

Grated zest from 1 organic lemon, optional

Organic honey, date honey, maple syrup or agave syrup

1 teaspoon blackberry liqueur (such as Crème de Cassis), optional

4 chilled organic kiwis, peeled and chopped into chunks

2 or 3 organic mint leaves

1 teaspoon lemon liqueur (such as Limoncello), optional

2 chilled organic mangoes, pitted, peeled and chopped into chunks

Organic pomegranate seeds, for garnish

DIRECTIONS

1. Using a handheld blender, puree the raspberries and the lemon zest until smooth. Mix in a few drops of honey and the blackberry liqueur until thoroughly combined. Pour the puree through a strainer and set aside.

2. Using the same handheld blender, puree the kiwi and the mint leaves until smooth. Mix in a few drops of honey and the lemon liqueur until thoroughly combined and set aside.

3. Process the mango until smooth and set aside.

4. Divide the fruit purees evenly among the five shot classes. You can add them all in the same order or in different orders. Garnish by sprinkling pomegranate seeds on top and serve immediately.

Makes 4 servings

This delicious combination of fresh berries, coconut cream and meringue is simply irresistible. It happens to be gluten-free too! Serve in a glass cup or jar—whatever you have on hand—just make sure it's transparent so your guests can see the gorgeous layers. If you make the meringue yourself (you can also use store-bought varieties), make sure you follow the principles of meringue-making; that is, use even quantities of egg yolks, sugar and confectioners' sugar. The meringues can be made in advance and stored for up to two weeks at room temperature, or two months in the freezer.

The coconut cream can be substituted with regular cream and you can use other berries instead of strawberries. For a really indulgent dessert, double the amount of cream.

INGREDIENTS

Meringue

4 medium organic free-range egg whites (about 4 ounces)

1 cup + 1 tablespoon organic brown cane sugar

1 cup organic cane confectioners' sugar

Coconut Cream

One 13½-ounce can organic coconut cream, chilled overnight

2 tablespoons organic cane confectioners' sugar

A few drops of organic pure vanilla extract or a few vanilla seeds

4 cups fresh organic strawberries

Fresh passion fruit coulis, for serving

Organic goji berries, chia seeds or nuts, for serving

DIRECTIONS

1. **Prepare the meringues:** Preheat the oven to 90° F and line a baking sheet with parchment paper.

2. Place the egg whites and brown sugar in a mixing bowl and set the bowl over a double boiler. Heat the double boiler over low heat and whisk the egg whites for a few moments until the sugar melts. Transfer the bowl to the mixer and continue whisking, this time using the whisk attachment, for about 4 minutes on medium speed, until the foam is stable and shiny.

3. Remove the bowl from the mixer and fold in the confectioners' sugar, folding gently until combined. Transfer the mixture to a piping bag and pipe little mounds onto the baking sheet. Alternatively, you could simply make little mounds of meringue using a small spoon. Bake the meringues for about 2 to 3 hours, until they are completely dry and can be removed easily from the baking sheet. Cool to room temperature.

4. **Prepare the coconut cream:** Ten minutes before you plan to begin, place the mixing bowl in the freezer to chill thoroughly.

5. Remove the can of coconut cream from the refrigerator and turn it upside-down on your work surface. Open the cream from the base. You'll notice that the solids in the cream have settled here during the chilling process. Remove these solids and set them aside for another use. Transfer the rest of the cream (the part that is still in a liquid form) to the chilled mixing bowl.

6. Add the confectioners' sugar and vanilla, and whip until light and fluffy. Serve immediately or chill until ready to serve.

7. If the whipped cream starts to lose volume, you may re-chill and then rewhip it.

8. **Assemble the dessert:** Just before serving, break several meringues into large chunks and distribute evenly among the serving glasses. Add a dollop of whipped cream to each serving and then top with fresh fruit. Serve immediately.

9. To make the dessert even more indulgent, serve with a fresh fruit coulis made from sour fruit such as passion fruit. For a healthier version, add goji berries, chia seeds or nuts.

Bars & Brownies

Peanut Butter Chocolate Squares (page 76)

Beet & Brazil Nut Brownies

Makes 16 brownies

In our opinion, beets are one of the world's most undervalued vegetables. In addition to their glorious color and natural sweetness, they are also very nutritious. When used in baking, they help to ensure a moist and juicy result.

INGREDIENTS

Salted water, for cooking

1 pound raw organic beets, peeled and chopped into large chunks

8 ounces organic dark chocolate, chopped

3½ ounces organic coconut oil or butter

3 large organic free-range eggs, room temperature

1¼ cups organic cane sugar

1½ teaspoons organic pure vanilla extract

¾ cup organic spelt or whole-wheat flour

3 tablespoons organic cocoa powder

Pinch of salt

1 cup coarsely chopped organic Brazil nuts

DIRECTIONS

1. In a large pot, heat the salted water until it boils. Add the beets and cook for about 40 minutes until completely soft. Drain off the water and transfer the beets to a food processor. Process until smooth.

2. Preheat the oven to 350°F and line an 8 x 10-inch baking pan with parchment paper.

3. Melt the chocolate using a double boiler or microwave, and then mix in the oil until smooth. In a small bowl, beat the eggs and sugar until light and creamy.

4. Add the melted chocolate and vanilla extract to the egg mixture, mixing until smooth. Beat in the beet puree until combined.

5. Whisk in the flour, cocoa and salt until the mixture is smooth. Pour the batter into the prepared baking pan and distribute the chopped Brazil nuts evenly on top.

6. Bake for 25 minutes until the top is crusty and there is a slight wobble underneath. Transfer to a wire rack and cool completely before cutting. To make clean, straight cuts, put the baking pan in the freezer for about 30 minutes before cutting, so that the brownie is partially frozen.

7. May be stored in an airtight container for up to 3 days.

Makes 12 bars

Granola bars are so popular in our families. They're a treat to eat at home and so easy to grab on the go. Store-bought granola are often filled with all sorts of ingredients that are anything but natural—but this homemade variety contains exactly what you want—with no surprises!

INGREDIENTS

1½ cups organic gluten-free old-fashioned rolled oats

½ cup organic brown cane sugar

⅓ cup organic spelt or whole-wheat flour

1 tablespoon organic chia or flax seeds

¼ teaspoon salt

¾ cup raw organic almonds

5 organic dates, pitted and chopped

½ cup organic pure tahini

¼ cup organic honey, date honey, maple syrup or date honey

5 tablespoons organic coconut oil, canola oil or melted organic butter

DIRECTIONS

1. Preheat the oven to 350°F and line a 9-inch square baking pan with parchment paper.

2. In a large bowl, combine the oats, sugar, flour, seeds, salt, almonds and dates.

3. In a separate bowl, combine the tahini, honey and oil.

4. Mix the tahini mixture into the oat mixture, mixing until combined.

5. Transfer the mixture to the pan and bake for 25 minutes until golden.

6. Remove from the oven and cool to room temperature, then cut into 4½ x 1½-inch bars.

7. May be stored in an airtight container for up to 3 days.

Pumpkin Spice Brownies

Makes 16 brownies

Thanks to the addition of pumpkin puree to this recipe, these brownies are moist, fudgy and healthy, too! You barely notice the pumpkin flavor, what with all the rich chocolate. The addition of the pumpkin pie spice highlights the flavor and makes the entire combination much more festive and fun. You can leave the pumpkin pie spice out altogether and children will never notice that they are eating pumpkin at all! We used organic butter for this recipe, but you can replace it with coconut oil or light olive oil if you like.

INGREDIENTS

7 ounces organic dark chocolate, coarsely chopped

7 ounces organic butter or coconut oil

3 large organic free-range eggs, room temperature

1¼ cups organic cane sugar

½ cup + 1 tablespoon whole-wheat flour

½ cup organic cocoa powder

Pinch of salt

8 ounces organic pumpkin puree

½ teaspoon organic pumpkin pie spice

DIRECTIONS

1. Preheat the oven to 350°F and line an 8-inch square baking pan with parchment paper.

2. Using a double boiler or microwave, melt the chocolate and butter, and mix until combined. At the same time, in a small bowl, beat the eggs and sugar until light and creamy.

3. Add the melted chocolate to the egg mixture, mixing until smooth. Whisk in the flour, cocoa and salt until the mixture is smooth, and then mix in the pumpkin puree and pumpkin pie spice. Transfer to the baking pan.

4. Bake for 25 minutes until the top is crusty and there is a slight wobble underneath. Transfer to a wire rack and cool completely before cutting. To make clean, straight cuts, put the baking pan in the freezer for about 30 minutes before cutting so that the brownie is partially frozen.

5. May be stored in an airtight container for up to 3 days.

Pumpkin Pecan Granola Bars

Makes 18 bars

The pumpkin in these granola bars makes them particularly moist. This can make cutting the bars into perfect rectangles a bit difficult, but our kids came up with a perfect alternative: arrange the granola in mounds rather than bars, and serve as deliciously oversized granola cookies!

INGREDIENTS

4 cups organic gluten-free old-fashioned rolled oats

½ cup organic coconut oil, canola oil or melted organic butter

½ cup organic maple syrup, date honey, honey or agave syrup

½ cup organic pumpkin puree

1 teaspoon organic pumpkin pie spice

¼ teaspoon salt

1 cup chopped raw organic pecans

¼ cup organic pumpkin seeds

DIRECTIONS

1. Preheat the oven to 350°F and line a 9-inch square baking pan with parchment paper.

2. Place the oats in a large bowl.

3. In a separate bowl, combine the oil, maple syrup, pumpkin puree, pumpkin pie spice and salt.

4. Add the pecans and pumpkin seeds, and mix well.

5. Add the oil mixture to the oats and stir until evenly coated.

6. Transfer the mixture to the pan and bake for 25 minutes until golden.

7. Remove from the oven and cool to room temperature, then cut into 4½ x 1-inch bars. If some of the pieces are still a bit moist, keep the oven set to 350°F and bake for another 10 to 15 minutes, until they are crunchy and stable.

8. May be stored in an airtight container for up to 3 days.

Carob Fudge Squares

Makes 48 squares

These delicious fudgy squares are easy to make and, unlike many fudge recipes, they don't require the use of a baking thermometer. All you do is melt, mix, chill, cut and devour. The ingredients are simple, too. You just need chocolate, carob spread and your favorite dried fruit or nuts. We've used pistachios and dried apricots, but you can replace these, according to your very own sweet tooth.

INGREDIENTS

10 ounces high-quality (70% cocoa) organic dark chocolate, coarsely chopped

12 ounces organic carob spread

1 cup roasted organic pistachios or hazelnuts

2 tablespoons organic dried apricots, cut into small chunks

2 tablespoons organic dried orange strips or crystallized ginger

2 tablespoons chopped organic raisins

¼ cup organic light raisins

¼ teaspoon organic cardamom powder, cinnamon or pure vanilla extract

DIRECTIONS

1. Line an 8 x 6-inch baking pan with parchment paper. Using a double boiler or microwave, melt the chocolate and then transfer to a large bowl.

2. Mix in the carob spread until thoroughly combined. Mix in the pistachios, apricots, orange strips, both types of raisins and cardamom.

3. Pour the mixture into the baking tray and flatten the top with a spatula. Transfer the tray to the refrigerator and chill for about 2 hours until the mixture hardens. Cut into 1-inch squares and serve.

4. May be stored in an airtight container for up to 3 days.

Hazelnut Espresso Meringue Bars

Makes 25 squares

Here's a lovely teatime treat that is gluten-free and dairy-free. It's perfectly accompanied by tea, coffee or milk.

INGREDIENTS

¾ pound organic hazelnut flour

2½ cups organic cane confectioners' sugar

4 large organic free-range egg whites

2 tablespoons fresh espresso

Grated zest from 1 organic orange or lemon

DIRECTIONS

1. Preheat the oven to 350°F and line a 10-inch baking pan with parchment paper.

2. In a large, heatproof mixing bowl, combine the hazelnut flour, confectioners' sugar, egg whites, espresso and orange zest. Place the bowl over a double boiler and heat, while stirring constantly, until the mixture is warm.

3. Transfer the bowl to the mixing stand and beat with the paddle attachment for about 5 minutes, until the mixture is thick and light.

4. Pour the mixture into the baking pan, flatten with a spatula and bake for about 30 minutes, until a hard cracked crust forms on top.

5. Remove from the oven and set aside for about 2 hours until completely cooled. Cut into 2-inch squares and serve.

6. May be refrigerated in an airtight container for up to 1 week.

Peanut Butter Chocolate Squares

Makes 36 squares

See photo page 64

These squares are gluten-free, dairy-free and have no eggs. They are a rich and juicy vegan treat. They are also easy to make and deliciously rewarding.

INGREDIENTS

½ cup organic peanut butter

3 tablespoons agave syrup

½ cup organic unsweetened applesauce

1 large ripe organic banana, mashed

6 tablespoons organic cocoa powder

¼ teaspoon sea salt

DIRECTIONS

1. Preheat the oven to 350°F and line an 8-inch square baking pan with parchment paper.

2. In a large bowl, combine the peanut butter, agave syrup, applesauce, banana, cocoa and salt.

3. Transfer the mixture to the baking pan and smooth the top with a spatula. Bake for about 20 minutes until solid, yet still moist. Cool to room temperature before cutting. Cut into 1-inch squares and serve.

4. May be stored in an airtight container for up to 3 days.

Hazelnut Chocolate Goji Fudge Squares

Makes 40 squares

These fudgy squares are much easier to make than ordinary fudge, and much healthier too! They feature an indulgent combination of chocolate, creamy nut spread and honey. You can replace the almonds with another favorite nut, if you like. The goji berries can be replaced with raisins or chopped dates.

INGREDIENTS

10½ ounces organic dark chocolate, coarsely chopped

6 ounces organic hazelnut spread, chocolate hazelnut spread, almond butter or peanut butter

¼ cup organic honey, date honey or maple syrup

1 cup toasted organic slivered almonds

¼ cup organic goji berries

¼ cup chopped dried organic citrus peel or another dried fruit

DIRECTIONS

1. Line an 8-inch brownie pan with parchment paper. Using a double boiler or microwave, melt the chocolate until smooth.

2. Mix in the hazelnut spread and mix until smooth.

3. Add the honey, almonds, goji berries and fruit, and mix until evenly combined.

4. Pour the mixture into the baking pan and refrigerate for about 4 hours until the mixture hardens.

5. Cut into small squares and serve.

6. May be refrigerated in an airtight container for about 2 weeks.

Sweet Date Salame

Makes 80 slices

This traditional Italian dessert is perfect for vegans. It contains no eggs, no dairy, and no gluten—just 100% natural goodness. Needless to say, it is also beautiful for serving at any meal or occasion. If you're not in a rush, you can toast the nuts in advance. The flavor will be better, though the nutritional value will be reduced.

INGREDIENTS

⅓ cup organic honey

½ pound soft organic dates, halved and pitted

1 cup raw organic walnuts

½ cup raw organic hazelnuts

½ cup raw organic cashews

1 cup raw organic pecans

½ teaspoon organic ground cinnamon

½ teaspoon organic rose water or a pinch of organic ground nutmeg +
¼ teaspoon organic ground cardamom

Pinch of salt

1 cup organic whole sesame seeds, for rolling

½ cup organic sesame seeds, for rolling

DIRECTIONS

1. In a medium saucepan, heat the honey over medium heat until it is almost boiling, and then mix in the dates. Cook, while stirring, until smooth.

2. Remove the mixture from the heat and mix in the walnuts, hazelnuts, cashews, pecans, cinnamon, rose water and salt. Mix until the nuts are evenly distributed and then set aside for a few minutes to cool.

3. Transfer the cooled mixture to the refrigerator and chill for about 30 minutes. In the meantime, place the whole and regular sesame seeds in a large flat dish.

4. Divide the chilled mixture into three even pieces. Roll each piece into a thick log shape and then roll each log in the sesame seeds.

5. Wrap the sesame-covered logs in plastic wrap and refrigerate until ready to serve. Cut the logs into thin slices just before serving.

6. May be stored in the refrigerator, wrapped and in an airtight container, for up to 2 weeks.

Jam Streusel Squares

Makes 20 squares

Who knew this traditional teatime treat could be so healthy? Made with gluten-free flour and organic jam, it's a great afternoon snack that even your Great Aunt Ida will love.

INGREDIENTS

1 cup gluten-free organic oat flour

⅔ cup organic almond flour

½ cup organic cane sugar

4 tablespoons organic rice flour

6 ounces organic butter, cold and cut into small cubes

11 ounces organic pure quince, apple or berry jam

DIRECTIONS

1. Line a 20-inch square baking pan with parchment paper.

2. In the bowl of a mixer, combine the oat flour, almond flour, sugar and rice flour until evenly combined. Add the butter, and pulse just until chunks form. You can also mix in the butter with your fingers.

3. Set aside ¾ cup of the crumble mixture in the freezer and pat the rest of it evenly in the base of the baking pan. Transfer the crust to the freezer and chill for about 1 hour until the dough hardens.

4. Preheat the oven to 350°F. Spread the jam on the chilled crust and then sprinkle the crumble mixture you set aside previously on top. If it isn't crumbly enough, use a grater to crumble it.

5. Transfer to the oven and bake for 40 minutes, or until the dough is golden. Chill completely and then slice into 1-inch squares.

6. May be stored in an airtight container for up to 1 week.

Sticks & Skewers

Banana Cake Pops with Cashew Coating (page 88)
Sweet Potato Cake Pops with Chocolate Coating (page 96)

Makes 8 pops

Make these gorgeous frozen pops by pressing chunks of real fruit into the frozen pop containers. Add fruit infusions or fresh fruit juice, freeze, and voilà!—you've got a gorgeous and refreshing treat that's healthy and fun!

Make sure that you pack the fruit quite closely together, since the frozen liquid is tea or juice, rather than syrup. This means these fruit pops will thaw faster than commercial frozen pops which have sugar (and therefore a slower thawing period).

INGREDIENTS

2 cups fresh fruit (such as strawberries, kiwi, plums, lychee and passion fruit), peeled, pitted and cut into 1-inch pieces

8 fresh mint leaves, sliced into strips

2 cups sweetened herb or fruit infusion, or freshly squeezed fruit juice

DIRECTIONS

1. Distribute the fruit pieces evenly among the ice-pop molds. Tuck the mint leaves in between the fruit pieces and then press the fruit firmly into the molds.

2. Pour the herb infusion into the molds and insert ice-pop sticks.

3. Transfer to the freezer and freeze for about 6 hours until solid. Serve directly from the freezer.

4. May be stored for up to 2 weeks.

Mango Lassi Frozen Pops

Makes 6 pops

These homemade frozen pops are inspired by the Lassi, a traditional Indian yogurt drink that is as refreshing as it is nutritious. The yogurt mixture can be seasoned with cardamom, ginger, almond milk, almond extract or coconut milk; you can also just use regular milk and vanilla extract.

INGREDIENTS

½ *organic mango, peeled and pitted*

6 *ounces organic plain yogurt*

½ *cup organic almond milk, coconut milk or dairy milk*

1 *tablespoon organic maple syrup, agave syrup, date honey or honey*

⅛ *teaspoon organic ground cardamom*

⅛ *teaspoon organic ground ginger*

½ *teaspoon organic pure vanilla extract*

DIRECTIONS

1. Place the mango in a food processor or use a handheld blender, and puree until smooth.

2. Distribute the pureed mango evenly among the ice-pop molds. Insert the ice-pop sticks into the mango puree, pressing them firmly into the middle of each mold. Transfer to the freezer and freeze until the mango solidifies.

3. In a small bowl, combine the yogurt with the milk until smooth. Add the syrup, cardamom, ginger and vanilla extract, mixing until blended.

4. Pour the yogurt mixture onto the frozen mango puree and return to the freezer. Freeze for at least 3 hours, until completely frozen. Serve directly from the freezer.

5. May be stored for up to 2 weeks.

Makes 55 cake pops

See photo page 82

INGREDIENTS

Banana Cupcakes

½ cup organic coconut oil or canola oil

1 cup organic brown cane sugar

1 teaspoon organic pure vanilla extract or ground cinnamon

2 large organic free-range eggs, room temperature

2 large ripe organic bananas, mashed

1 cup organic spelt or whole-wheat flour

1 cup gluten-free organic oat flour

2 teaspoons organic baking powder

3 tablespoons organic date spread

1 ounce organic dark chocolate, coarsely chopped

Cashew Coating

½ cup raw organic cashews, soaked overnight in water

3 tablespoons organic honey, date honey, maple syrup or agave syrup

1 teaspoon organic pure vanilla extract

⅓ cup organic almond milk, cashew milk, rice milk or water

½ cup organic cocoa butter chips

2 ounces toasted organic shredded coconut, for topping

Believe it or not, these gourmet treats are also good for you. They're made with a moist banana cake made with ground oats rather than flour and a creamy cashew coating. The banana cupcakes rise a bit less than most other cupcakes, but since you'll be crumbling them anyway, that doesn't matter. As for the coating, it's a versatile vegan coating with a neutral flavor that can be flavored with extract or dipped in toasted coconut, chopped nuts or cocoa powder.

If you've never made cake pops before, see How to Make Cake Pops on page 11 for more tips. Before you start making this recipe, make sure you have 55 lollipop sticks and a Styrofoam block on hand. Also, clear out room in your freezer so that the cake pops can stand upright as they chill.

DIRECTIONS

1. Prepare the cupcakes: Preheat the oven to 350°F and line a cupcake pan with paper liners.

2. In an electric mixer fitted with the paddle attachment, beat the oil, sugar and vanilla extract until smooth and light. Add the eggs, one at a time, mixing thoroughly after each addition. Add the bananas and beat for about 1 minute.

3. In a separate bowl, sift the flours and baking powder until combined. Transfer the flour mixture to the wet mixture, folding just until the texture is smooth and creamy.

4. Spoon the batter into the cupcake liners until three-quarters full and bake for about 15 minutes, or until a toothpick inserted in the center comes out dry. Transfer to a wire rack and cool to room temperature.

5. Remove the cupcakes from their paper liners and transfer to a food processor. Process until crumbly.

6. Transfer the crumbled cake to a large mixing bowl. Gradually mix in the date spread, combining until the mixture is smooth and can be rolled into

(continued on page 90)

(continued from page 88)

balls. If the mixture is too moist, the balls will sweat through the cashew coating. If the mixture is too dry, the balls won't hold their shape. You'll know the mixture is the right texture when you can roll it with your hands without getting your hands dirty.

7. Roll the crumbled cake mixture into ¾-inch balls and arrange on a baking sheet. Using a double boiler or microwave, melt the chocolate until smooth. Dip the top $\frac{1}{10}$ inch of each lollipop stick into the melted chocolate and then insert it into a cake ball. This chocolate will act like glue on the inside of the cake ball to help it stay in place. Transfer the cake balls with the sticks to the freezer and chill for 30 minutes.

8. While the cake balls are chilling, prepare the coating: Drain the water from the cashews and transfer the cashews to a food processor or blender. Add the honey, vanilla extract and milk, and blend until smooth.

9. Using a double boiler or microwave, melt the cocoa butter chips. Mix until smooth and then mix into the cashew mixture until evenly combined. Transfer the cashew coating to a tall cup that is slightly wider than a cake ball. Place the toasted coconut in a similarly sized cup.

10. One by one, dip the cake balls into the cashew coating and then into the toasted coconut. Insert the bottom of the stick into the Styrofoam block. Transfer the dipped cake balls to the freezer and chill for about 2 hours, until the coating hardens.

11. After the cake pops have frozen, they can be laid on their side. Store frozen in an airtight container until ready to serve. Remove from the freezer about 20 minutes before serving.

12. May be stored in the freezer in an airtight container for up to 2 weeks.

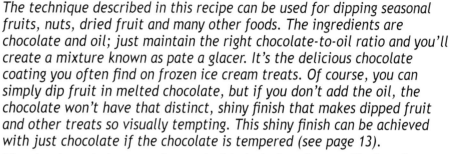

v **df** **gf**   *Chocolate Dipped Fruit*

Makes 1 pound dipped fruit

See photo page 93

The technique described in this recipe can be used for dipping seasonal fruits, nuts, dried fruit and many other foods. The ingredients are chocolate and oil; just maintain the right chocolate-to-oil ratio and you'll create a mixture known as pate a glacer. It's the delicious chocolate coating you often find on frozen ice cream treats. Of course, you can simply dip fruit in melted chocolate, but if you don't add the oil, the chocolate won't have that distinct, shiny finish that makes dipped fruit and other treats so visually tempting. This shiny finish can be achieved with just chocolate if the chocolate is tempered (see page 13).

The simple technique can be used with dark chocolate, milk chocolate or white chocolate—just make sure you use excellent quality chocolate. You can flavor the chocolate with grated orange or lemon zests, pumpkin pie spice, cardamom, cinnamon or vanilla extract.

A short note about the fruit: Wash it first and then make sure it is completely dry before you dip it. It's important for the fruit to be dry because the chocolate coating won't stick if the fruit is damp.

After dipping the fruit in the chocolate, you can dip the fruit in chopped nuts or toasted grated coconut, or drizzle on melted chocolate of a different color. Transfer to the refrigerator or freezer to harden.

INGREDIENTS

1 pound fresh organic kiwis, bananas or strawberries

10½ ounces high-quality organic chocolate, cut into chunks

2 tablespoons organic coconut oil or canola oil

2 tablespoons organic chopped nuts or toasted organic shredded coconut, optional

DIRECTIONS

1. Line a baking sheet with parchment paper and make room in your freezer or refrigerator.

2. Wash the fruit and dry it well. If you are using large fruit, such as bananas or kiwis, cut them into thick slices. If you'll be inserting sticks into the fruit, first make a small slit in the fruit with a paring knife, so that the stick will have no trouble sliding in.

3. Using a double boiler or microwave, melt the chocolate. Add the oil and mix until smooth. Transfer the chocolate mixture to a narrow cup that is just large enough to dip the fruit slices into.

(continued on page 92)

(continued from page 91)

4. Dip the fruit into the chocolate. If the layer of chocolate is too thin, place the dipped fruit in the freezer or refrigerator for a few moments and then dip it again to make a second layer.

5. If you like, dip the chocolate-dipped fruit in chopped nuts or sprinkle with coconut before the chocolate hardens.

6. Place the dipped fruit on the baking sheet and transfer to the refrigerator or freezer to chill until the chocolate hardens. Serve on the same day.

Chocolate Truffle Pops

Makes 25 truffles

See photo page 95

This elegant dessert, made from coconut cream and chocolate, is an excellent topping for so many treats. The flavor of the coconut cream is quite mild when paired with the chocolate, so it's easy to enhance with other flavors. Try citrus zests, brandy or coffee liqueurs, or pure vanilla or almond extract.

Truffles that haven't been dipped in coating may be frozen in an airtight container for up to 1 month. They are great to have on hand in case unexpected guests drop by. Once you've rolled the chocolates, dip them in tempered chocolate (page 13) or pate a glacer (recipe below) to create a hard and shiny chocolate coating.

If you're short on time or don't want the chocolate coating, simply roll the truffles in an elegant topping, such as organic cocoa powder, confectioners' cane sugar, shredded coconut or chopped nuts.

For maximum presentation, we've inserted lollipop sticks into the balls just before serving. You can also use cinnamon sticks or candy canes, or serve the truffles directly on an elegant serving dish.

(continued on page 94)

Chocolate Dipped Fruit

(continued from page 92)

INGREDIENTS

Truffles

1 cup organic coconut cream

¼ teaspoon sea salt

14 ounces high-quality organic dark chocolate, coarsely chopped

¾ ounces organic cocoa or dairy butter

¼ teaspoon organic flavoring (such as grated orange zest, natural almond extract, natural coffee extract, ground cardamom, vanilla extract, brandy, amaretto, coffee liqueur or rum)

Coating

10½ ounces organic dark chocolate, coarsely chopped

2 tablespoons organic coconut oil or canola oil

Organic chopped nuts, shredded coconut, cocoa or confectioners' sugar, for topping, optional

DIRECTIONS

1. Prepare the truffles: Pour the cream and salt into a small pot and bring almost to a boil. Using a microwave or double boiler, melt the chocolate. Mix the coconut cream into the melted chocolate until smooth.

2. Add the cocoa butter and the flavoring, and stir until mixture is smooth.

3. Transfer the mixture to the refrigerator and chill for about 1 hour, or until the mixture is stable enough to shape into balls.

4. Transfer the chilled mixture to a pastry bag and pipe into 1-inch mounds. Wearing disposable gloves, roll the mounds into balls.

5. Insert a lollipop stick into each ball, place on a baking sheet and return to the freezer for about 1 hour until the balls harden.

6. Prepare the coating: Line a baking sheet with parchment paper. Using a microwave or double boiler, melt the chocolate. Mix in the oil until smooth. Transfer the mixture to a tall narrow glass that you can easily dip the truffles into.

7. Holding the truffles by the lollipop stick, dip them into the chocolate mixture, one at a time. Tap the stick gently to get rid of excess chocolate and arrange on the lined baking sheet. Transfer to the freezer to harden.

8. If you want to top the coated balls with chopped nuts or shredded coconut, do so before the chocolate topping has hardened. If you want to cover the balls with cocoa or confectioners' sugar, do so after the coating has hardened, just before serving.

9. Store the truffles in an airtight container in the freezer until ready to serve. May be frozen in an airtight container for up to 1 month.

Sweet Potato Cake Pops with Chocolate Coating

Makes 70 cake pops

See photo page 82

These delicious treats are made with crumbled sweet potato cupcakes mixed with soft white cheese, soft tofu or date spread. Dipped in chocolate and presented on a pop, they are a deliciously indulgent—not to mention interesting and impressive—treat.

If you've never made cake pops before, see How to Make Cake Pops on page 11 for more tips. Before you start making this recipe, make sure you have 70 lollipop sticks and a Styrofoam block on hand. Also clear out room in your freezer so that the cake pops can stand upright as they chill.

INGREDIENTS

Sweet Potato Cupcakes

3½ ounces organic butter

¾ cup organic brown cane sugar

1 teaspoon organic ground cinnamon

¼ teaspoon organic ground ginger

Pinch of organic ground nutmeg

8 ounces cooked organic sweet potato, mashed lightly with a fork

2 large organic free-range eggs, room temperature

1 cup organic spelt or whole-wheat flour

1 teaspoon organic baking powder

¼ cup soft white cheese, soft tofu or date spread

1 ounce organic dark chocolate, coarsely chopped

DIRECTIONS

1. Prepare the cupcakes: Preheat the oven to 350°F and line a cupcake pan with paper liners.

2. In an electric mixer fitted with the paddle attachment, beat the butter, sugar, cinnamon, ginger and nutmeg until light and airy. Mix in the sweet potato until the texture is smooth, and then add the eggs, one at a time, mixing thoroughly after each addition.

3. In a separate bowl, sift the flour and baking powder until combined. Transfer the flour mixture to the wet mixture, folding just until the texture is smooth and creamy.

4. Spoon the batter into the cupcake liners until three-quarters full and bake for about 15 minutes, or until a toothpick inserted in the center comes out dry. Transfer to a wire rack and cool to room temperature.

5. Remove the cupcakes from their paper liners and transfer to a food processor. Process until crumbly.

6. Transfer the crumbled cupcakes to a large mixing bowl. Gradually mix in the white cheese, combining until the mixture is smooth and can be rolled into balls. If the mixture is too moist, the balls will sweat through

Organic Sweets and Treats

Chocolate Coating

11 ounces organic dark chocolate, coarsely chopped

2 tablespoons organic coconut oil or canola oil

the chocolate coating. If the mixture is too dry, the balls won't hold their shape. You'll know the mixture is the right texture when you can roll it with your hands without getting your hands dirty.

7. Roll the crumbled cake mixture into ¾-inch balls and arrange on a baking sheet. Using a double boiler or microwave, melt the chocolate until smooth. Dip the top $\frac{1}{10}$ inch of each lollipop stick into the melted chocolate and then insert it into a cake ball. This chocolate will act like glue on the inside of the cake ball to help it stay in place. Transfer the cake balls with the sticks to the freezer and chill for 30 minutes.

8. While the cake balls are chilling, prepare the coating: Using a double boiler or microwave, melt the chocolate. Mix in the oil until the texture is smooth and suitable for dipping. Transfer the chocolate coating to a tall cup that is slightly wider than a cake ball.

9. One by one, dip the cake balls into the chocolate coating and then insert the bottom of the stick into a Styrofoam block. Transfer the dipped cake balls to the freezer and chill for about 2 hours, until the coating hardens.

10. After the cake pops have frozen, they can be laid on their side and stored in an airtight container until ready to serve. Remove from the freezer about 20 minutes before serving.

11. May be stored in the freezer in an airtight container for up to 2 weeks.

Sticks & Skewers

Blueberry Yogurt Pops

Makes 6 pops

These frozen fruit pops taste as good as they look. They have all the fun of a frozen summer treat and contain only healthful ingredients, starting with fresh blueberries and ending with organic plain yogurt.

INGREDIENTS

36 organic fresh blueberries

2 ounces fresh or frozen organic blueberries

6 ounces organic plain yogurt

½ cup organic almond milk, coconut milk or dairy milk

1 tablespoon organic honey, date honey, maple syrup or agave syrup

½ teaspoon organic pure vanilla extract or grated zest from ½ organic lemon

DIRECTIONS

1. Place 6 whole blueberries in each ice-pop mold or cup.

2. Place the remaining 2 ounces of blueberries in a food processor or use a handheld blender, and puree until smooth.

3. In a medium bowl, mix the pureed blueberries with the yogurt, milk, honey and vanilla extract until evenly combined. Distribute the mixture evenly among the ice-pop cups and insert ice-pop sticks.

4. Transfer to the freezer and freeze for at least 3 hours until completely frozen.

5. Just before serving, dip each ice-pop mold into boiling water for a moment or two to heat the outside of the mold and loosen it from the yogurt pop.

6. May be stored in the freezer in an airtight container for up to 2 weeks.

Serves 10

INGREDIENTS

¼ *large seedless watermelon, thoroughly chilled*

10 ounces organic feta cheese

This showstopper dessert relies on a simple technique that can be used with diverse ingredients. Inspired by the wonderful Greek combination of salty and sweet, you can keep the salty/sweet combination by replacing the watermelon with sweet red tomatoes or sweet melon.

When serving watermelon, chill it thoroughly for best flavor and cut it as close as possible to serving time. Make sure you use salty feta cheese, and feel free to enhance with fresh basil or mint leaves.

DIRECTIONS

1. Slice the watermelon and feta cheese into thin slices.

2. Using flower or triangle cookie cutters, cut the watermelon and cheese slices.

3. Arrange the watermelon and cheese slices as desired. If you are making the flowers, insert lollipop sticks. Serve immediately.

Cookies & Petits Fours

Thumbprint Spelt Cookies (page 121)

Makes 20 cookies

These cookies, made without any flour or eggs, are a perfect accompaniment for tea, coffee or milk. If you're not a fan of coconut, replace it with coarsely chopped walnuts or almonds.

INGREDIENTS

7 ounces organic peanut butter

¾ cup organic cane sugar

2 tablespoons water

½ teaspoon baking soda

Pinch of salt

1 cup chopped organic dark chocolate or organic chocolate chips

1 ounce organic shredded coconut

DIRECTIONS

1. Preheat the oven to 320°F and line a baking sheet with parchment paper.

2. In a large bowl, combine the peanut butter, sugar and water until smooth and evenly mixed.

3. Mix in the baking soda, salt, chocolate and coconut until the mixture is evenly mixed and a bit sticky.

4. Wet your hands a bit and roll the dough into ½-inch balls, then arrange the balls on the baking sheet.

5. Bake the cookies for 13 to 16 minutes, or until they are golden and firm around the edges but still soft on the inside. Cool to room temperature before serving.

6. May be stored in an airtight container for up to 1 week.

Sesame Almond Quinoa Cookies

Makes 25 cookies

These crispy-on-the-outside cookies melt in your mouth, with a combination of textures that just can't be beaten. They are rich in flavor even though they don't have any wheat flour or eggs. For variety, we suggest covering half of the cookies in quinoa grains and the other half in sesame seeds, but if you're missing one of these toppings, dip them all in same one.

INGREDIENTS

1½ cups organic quinoa flour

½ cup organic cane sugar or organic brown cane sugar

⅓ cup organic almond oil or canola oil

½ cup organic almond spread, hazelnut spread or organic pure tahini

Grated zest from 1 organic lemon or lime

½ cup organic sesame seeds, for coating

½ cup organic quinoa grains, for coating

DIRECTIONS

1. Preheat the oven to 330°F and line a baking sheet with parchment paper.

2. In a large mixing bowl, combine the flour, sugar, oil, almond spread and lemon zest. Mix until thoroughly combined.

3. Shape the dough into 1-inch balls and flatten each ball gently between your fingers.

4. Place the sesame seeds and the quinoa grains in two small shallow dishes. Dip each flattened ball of dough in one of the dishes so that both sides are coated with seeds or grains, and arrange them on the baking sheet.

5. Bake for 20 to 25 minutes until the cookies are lightly golden. The cookies will be soft when you take them out of the oven, but will harden as they cool. Serve at room temperature.

6. May be stored in an airtight container for up to 2 weeks.

Chocolate-Covered Stuffed Dates

Makes 12 stuffed dates

These treats are a powerhouse of flavor and nutrition. Hidden inside the delicious chocolate filling are healthy goji berries and delicious Brazil nuts.

INGREDIENTS

12 large organic dates, pitted

12 organic Brazil nuts, shelled

12 organic goji berries

3 tablespoons organic cocoa butter or coconut oil

3 tablespoons organic cocoa powder

½ cup finely ground organic pistachios

DIRECTIONS

1. Line a baking sheet with parchment paper and set aside. Stuff each date with 1 Brazil nut and 1 goji berry, and set aside.

2. Using a double boiler or microwave, melt the cocoa butter until smooth. Mix in the cocoa powder until smooth and shiny.

3. Dip one end of a stuffed date into the chocolate mixture and then dip in the pistachios. Place on the baking sheet to harden.

4. Repeat step 3 to dip each of the dates in the chocolate and then in the pistachios. Set aside to harden and then serve. May be stored in an airtight container for up to 1 week.

Tahini Sorghum Cookies

Makes 25 cookies

Sorghum is a gluten-free grain that's a staple in India and Africa. High in protein, iron and dietary fiber, it adds great flavor too.

INGREDIENTS

1½ cups sorghum flour

¾ cup organic brown cane sugar or organic cane sugar

⅓ cup organic almond oil or canola oil

½ cup organic pure tahini

Sesame seeds, for rolling

DIRECTIONS

1. Preheat the oven to 330°F and line a baking sheet with parchment paper.

2. In a large bowl, combine the flour, sugar, oil and tahini until a dough forms.

3. Roll the dough into small balls, flatten the balls with a fork, and then dip both sides in the sesame seeds.

4. Arrange the cookies on the baking sheet and bake for about 20 minutes, until lightly golden. The cookies will be soft when they come out of the oven, but will harden after cooling.

5. Serve at room temperature. May be stored in an airtight container for up to 2 weeks.

Hazelnut Orange Quinoa Cookies

Makes 25 cookies

The combination of tangy orange zest and smooth hazelnut paste is simply lovely. Topped with quinoa grains, these cookies are perfect for teatime or anytime.

INGREDIENTS

1½ cups organic quinoa flour

½ cup organic cane sugar or organic brown cane sugar

⅓ cup organic almond oil or canola oil

½ cup organic hazelnut spread

Grated zest from 1 organic orange

½ cup organic quinoa grains, for coating

DIRECTIONS

1. Preheat the oven to 330°F and line a baking sheet with parchment paper.

2. In a large mixing bowl, combine the flour, sugar, oil, hazelnut spread and orange zest. Mix until thoroughly combined.

3. Shape the dough into 1-inch balls and flatten each ball gently between your fingers.

4. Place the quinoa grains in a small shallow dish and dip each flattened ball of dough into the grains so that both sides are coated.

5. Arrange the cookies on the baking sheet and bake for 20 to 25 minutes, until the cookies are lightly golden. The cookies will be soft when you take them out of the oven, but will harden as they cool.

6. Serve at room temperature. May be stored in an airtight container for up to 2 weeks.

Tahini Almond Clusters

Makes 20 clusters

These gluten-free cookies are really simple to make. They require just a few ingredients and are easily mixed by hand. They taste so wonderful that you'll find yourself making them again and again. It's also worth mentioning that tahini is rich in iron with a wonderful, lightly sweet flavor.

INGREDIENTS

2 cups organic slivered almonds

1 cup organic cane sugar

1 tablespoon organic honey, date honey, maple syrup or agave syrup

1 tablespoon organic pure tahini

1 large organic free-range egg white

DIRECTIONS

1. Preheat the oven to 260°F and line a baking sheet with parchment paper.

2. Place the almonds, sugar, honey, tahini and egg white in a large bowl and mix gently until the almonds are evenly coated. Take care that you don't break the almonds while mixing.

3. Spoon small, evenly spaced mounds of dough onto the baking sheet and bake for about 30 minutes, until golden.

4. Remove from the oven and cool to room temperature before serving.

5. May be stored in an airtight container for up to 7 days.

Date Truffles

These truffles look just like the ones made from chocolate, but they're actually made with date puree that's enriched with a different flavoring every time. Incredibly versatile, they can be made with a variety of nuts, dried fruit and spices, and then rolled in a range of toppings. In other words, the possibilities are virtually endless! Try making two or three types of truffles for a beautiful and delicious variety.

We recommend wearing disposal gloves when rolling these truffles so that the date puree doesn't stick to your fingers. Also, we suggest storing the truffles in the refrigerator—even though they are dairy-free—to make sure they stay stable.

Choose dates that are quite soft, since they'll turn into a sticky puree quite quickly when mixed. If the dates you've chosen don't puree easily, put them into a food processor and pulse a few times until smooth.

Walnut and Raisin Truffles

Makes 40 truffles

INGREDIENTS

1 pound soft organic dates (such as medjool), halved and pitted

1½ cups finely chopped organic walnuts

1 cup finely chopped organic raisins

2 ounces organic whole-wheat biscuits, finely chopped

¼ to ½ teaspoon organic ground cinnamon

½ cup whole organic sesame seeds or whole sesame / regular sesame mixture, for rolling

DIRECTIONS

1. Wear disposable gloves or lightly oil your hands. Place the dates in a large bowl and knead with your fingers until soft. If the dates don't soften enough, transfer them to a food processor and pulse a few times until pureed.

2. Mix in the walnuts, raisins, biscuits and cinnamon, mixing until evenly combined. Pour the sesame seeds into a small shallow dish.

3. Roll the mixture into balls and then roll the balls in the sesame seeds until evenly covered.

4. Arrange on a serving platter and refrigerate until truffles are solid. May be stored in an airtight container in the refrigerator for up to 2 weeks.

Ginger Truffles

Makes 40 truffles

INGREDIENTS

½ pound soft organic dates (such as medjool), halved and pitted

7 ounces roasted organic cashews, finely chopped

3½ ounces organic crystallized ginger, finely chopped

½ cup raw or toasted organic shredded coconut, for rolling

DIRECTIONS

1. Wear disposable gloves or lightly oil your hands. Place the dates in a large bowl and knead with your fingers until soft. If the dates don't soften enough, transfer them to a food processor and pulse a few times until pureed.

2. Mix in the cashews and ginger until evenly combined. Pour the coconut into a separate shallow dish.

3. Roll the date mixture into balls and then roll the balls in the coconut until evenly covered.

4. Arrange on a serving platter and refrigerate until truffles are solid. May be stored in an airtight container in the refrigerator for up to 2 weeks.

Goji Berry Truffles

Makes 40 truffles

INGREDIENTS

1 pound soft organic dates (such as medjool), halved and pitted

7 ounces organic pecans, roasted and finely chopped

3½ ounces organic goji berries

½ cup finely chopped organic almonds, for rolling

DIRECTIONS

1. Wear disposable gloves or lightly oil your hands. Place the dates in a large bowl and knead with your fingers until soft. If the dates don't soften enough, transfer them to a food processor and pulse a few times until pureed.

2. Mix in the pecans and goji berries until evenly combined. Pour the chopped almonds into a separate shallow dish.

3. Roll the date mixture into balls and then roll the balls in the almonds until evenly covered.

4. Arrange on a serving platter and refrigerate until truffles are solid. May be stored in an airtight container in the refrigerator for up to 2 weeks.

Hazelnut, Biscuit and Cocoa Truffles

Makes 40 truffles

INGREDIENTS

1 pound soft organic dates (such as medjool), halved and pitted

7 ounces organic hazelnuts, roasted and finely chopped

7 ounces organic whole-wheat biscuits, finely chopped

½ cup organic cocoa powder, for rolling

DIRECTIONS

1. Wear disposable gloves or lightly oil your hands. Place the dates in a large bowl and knead with your fingers until soft. If the dates don't soften enough, transfer them to a food processor and pulse a few times until pureed.

2. Mix in the hazelnuts and biscuits until evenly combined. Pour the cocoa into a separate shallow dish.

3. Roll the date mixture into balls and then roll the balls in the cocoa until evenly covered.

4. Arrange on a serving platter and refrigerate until truffles are solid. May be stored in an airtight container in the refrigerator for up to 2 weeks.

Almond Seed Clusters

Makes 40 clusters

These cookies have no flour or dairy products—just nuts, seeds, egg whites and sugar. Easy and quick to make, they are great for bringing on picnics and hikes, or for packing in school lunches. A healthy alternative to run-of-the mill granola bars.

INGREDIENTS

2 large organic free-range egg whites

¾ cup + 2 tablespoons organic cane confectioners' sugar

3 cups organic slivered almonds

4 tablespoons mixed organic seeds (such as sunflower, pumpkin, sesame and flaxseed)

DIRECTIONS

1. Preheat the oven to 330°F and line a baking sheet with parchment paper.

2. In a large mixing bowl, whisk together the egg whites and sugar, until the mixture is light but not too airy. Add the almonds and mix until they are evenly coated with the egg mixture. Add the seeds and mix, until they are thoroughly integrated into the mixture.

3. Use a tablespoon to drop the mixture into evenly spaced 1-inch balls on the baking sheet. Bake for about 15 minutes until the cookies are golden.

4. Let the cookies cool to room temperature and then serve.

5. May be stored in an airtight container for up to 1 week.

Seven-Nut Baklava

Makes one 10-inch pan

This Mediterranean delight is made with coconut oil rather than butter, and with maple and agave syrup instead of honey. It has lots of crunch and flavor, thanks to the combination of nuts and fragrant herbs, including orange blossom, cinnamon and cardamom. If you don't like the spice combination suggested below, try a more familiar flavoring, such as cinnamon and nutmeg, or cinnamon and orange zest.

Phyllo dough is thin and quite delicate; it starts drying out as soon as it comes in contact with air. For this reason, it's important to brush it immediately with oil or cover it with a damp cloth while you're working with it.

INGREDIENTS

Baklava

15 sheets phyllo dough

5 cups raw organic nuts (such as hazelnuts, pistachios, almonds, walnuts, cashews, pecans and peanuts)

1½ teaspoons ground cinnamon

¼ cup organic coconut oil, canola oil, olive oil or melted organic butter, plus more for greasing

Syrup

1½ cups water

1 cup organic maple syrup

½ cup agave syrup

1 cinnamon stick

Juice from ½ organic lemon

DIRECTIONS

1. **Prepare the baklava:** Preheat the oven to 350°F and grease a 10-inch square pan with oil.

2. Remove the frozen phyllo from the freezer and allow it to thaw on the countertop for about 20 minutes. In the meantime, place the nuts in the bowl of a food processor and pulse until coarsely chopped. Stir in the cinnamon.

3. Unwrap the thawed phyllo and lay the sheets flat on your work surface. If necessary, trim them to fit your pan, using a sharp knife.

4. Remove 5 phyllo sheets from the stack and cover the rest with a damp cloth. Working quickly, brush the top sheet with oil and lay it in the bottom of the pan. Repeat with the other four sheets of phyllo, brushing each one separately and laying them in a stack in the bottom of the pan.

5. Cover the phyllo sheets in the pan with about half of the mixed nuts, spreading them evenly with the back of a spoon.

6. Remove another 5 sheets of phyllo from the covered stack and repeat step 4, brushing each sheet with oil and then laying it in the pan, this time

(continued on page 120)

(continued from page 118)

10 cardamom pods or grated zest from 1 organic orange or lemon

½ to ¼ teaspoon organic orange blossom or rose water extract

on top of the nut filling. Cover with the remaining half of the mixed nuts, spreading them evenly with the back of a spoon. Uncover the last five sheets of phyllo pastry, brush with oil, and stack on top of the nut filling. Brush oil on the top sheet of phyllo as well.

7. Using a sharp knife, cut a diagonal pattern in the baklava. Make sure the knife cuts all the way to the bottom of the pan.

8. Transfer the pan to the oven and bake for 25 to 30 minutes until golden.

9. **In the meantime, prepare the syrup:** In a small saucepan, combine the water, maple syrup, agave syrup, cinnamon stick, lemon juice and cardamom pods. Bring to a boil, reduce heat to low, and then cook for about 10 minutes, until a fragrant and thick syrup forms. Pour the syrup through a fine mesh strainer to remove the whole spices, and then mix in the flavoring extract. Keep warm.

10. Remove the baklava from the oven and run a knife through the cuts to make sure that they are still open. Spoon the syrup over the baklava while it is still warm and then let it cool at room temperature for about 30 minutes. Serve at room temperature.

11. May be stored in an airtight container for up to 2 weeks.

Thumbprint Spelt Cookies

Makes 50 cookies

See photo page 102

No matter how modern the world gets, there's nothing quite as comforting as a jam-filled thumbprint cookie. Make this version with spelt flour rather than white flour and add delicious organic jam.

INGREDIENTS

2 cups organic spelt or whole-wheat flour

⅔ cup organic brown cane confectioners' sugar

5½ ounces cold organic butter, cut into cubes

⅓ cup organic coconut oil, canola oil or grape seed oil

⅓ cup organic jam, for filling

DIRECTIONS

1. Preheat the oven to 320°F and line a baking sheet with parchment paper.

2. In a food processor, combine the flour, sugar and butter cubes. Pulse until the mixture is crumbly. Add the oil and then pulse just until a smooth dough forms.

3. Roll the dough into 1-inch balls and arrange on the baking sheet. Make sure you leave some space between each ball so they have room to spread as they bake.

4. Press your fingertip into the top of each ball to make a small indentation and then transfer to the oven and bake for about 10 minutes.

5. Remove the cookies from the oven and press in the indentation a bit with the back of a spoon (it will have risen a bit during the baking). Drop ½ teaspoon of jam into each indentation and then return the cookies to the oven to bake for another 10 minutes, until the jam melts and the edges of the cookies are golden. Transfer to a wire rack and cool before serving.

6. May be stored in an airtight container at room temperature for up to 1 week.

Banana Phyllo Cigars

Makes 12 cigars

This impressive dish combines a symphony of flavors and textures: crispy phyllo, smooth chocolate and crunchy walnuts. Phyllo dough is thin and quite delicate; it starts drying out as soon as it comes in contact with air. For this reason, it's important to brush it immediately with oil or cover it with a damp cloth while you're working with it.

INGREDIENTS

Phyllo Cigars

6 sheets phyllo dough

3 large ripe organic bananas, chopped into small cubes

½ cup coarsely chopped organic walnuts

½ cup organic coconut oil, canola oil, olive oil or melted organic butter

¼ cup organic honey, date honey, maple syrup or agave syrup

Chocolate Sauce

1 cup coarsely chopped organic dark chocolate

¾ cup organic coconut cream

1 to 2 tablespoons organic honey, date honey, maple syrup or agave syrup

DIRECTIONS

1. **Prepare the phyllo cigars:** Preheat the oven to 350°F and line a baking pan with parchment paper.

2. Remove the frozen phyllo from the freezer and allow it to thaw on the countertop for about 20 minutes. In the meantime, combine the chopped bananas and walnuts in a small bowl.

3. Unwrap the thawed phyllo and lay 1 sheet flat on your work surface. Brush the sheet with oil and then lay another sheet of phyllo on top. Brush this sheet with oil and lay another sheet of phyllo on top.

4. Cut the stacked phyllo sheets in half lengthwise, and then cut each half into three rectangular strips. (Each strip should be about 4 x 6 inches.)

5. Spread about 1 tablespoon of the banana mixture along one long edge of each phyllo strip, leaving about ½ inch on the top and bottom without filling. Drizzle honey on top.

6. Roll each phyllo strip into a cigar as follows: first, make one complete roll of phyllo around the filling; then, tuck in the top and bottom edge and complete the roll. Arrange the phyllo cigars on the baking sheet, seam side down.

7. Repeat these steps to roll the rest of the cigars. Bake for about 15 minutes until the cigars are golden. Remove from the oven and set aside to cool.

8. **Prepare the chocolate sauce:** Using a double boiler or microwave, melt the chocolate.

9. In a small saucepan, bring the coconut cream just to a boil and then pour over the chocolate. Mix with a whisk until smooth. Mix in the honey. Drizzle the warm chocolate syrup on the warm phyllo cigars and serve.

Cakes & Quick Breads

Chunky Apple Muffins (page 130)

Banana Nut Bread

Makes 1 loaf

This delicious cake is made with hazelnut butter, but you can also make it with almond butter or coconut oil. This recipe is dairy-free, but can be made with melted dairy butter if you prefer. For a sweeter result, replace the nuts with 7 chopped dates or ½ cup organic chocolate chips.

INGREDIENTS

3 large ripe organic bananas, mashed

⅓ cup organic hazelnut butter, almond butter or coconut oil

1 large organic free-range egg, room temperature

½ cup organic unsweetened applesauce

½ cup + 1 teaspoon organic cane sugar

½ teaspoon + ¼ teaspoon ground cinnamon

1 teaspoon organic pure vanilla extract

¼ teaspoon salt

2 cups organic spelt or whole-wheat flour

1 teaspoon baking soda

½ cup mixed organic nuts

DIRECTIONS

1. Preheat the oven to 350°F. Grease a 9 x 5-inch loaf pan and line it with parchment paper.

2. In a large mixing bowl, combine the bananas, butter, egg, applesauce, ½ cup sugar, ½ teaspoon cinnamon, vanilla and salt, until well combined.

3. In a separate bowl, sift together the flour and the baking soda.

4. Add the flour mixture to the banana mixture, mixing just until combined, and then transfer to the loaf pan.

5. In a small bowl, combine the nuts, remaining 1 teaspoon of sugar and remaining ¼ teaspoon of cinnamon and then distribute evenly on top of the loaf.

6. Bake for about 45 minutes, until the cake is stable and golden, and a toothpick inserted into the middle comes out dry with crumbs. Let the loaf cool for at least 10 minutes and then serve.

7. May be stored in an airtight container for up to 3 days.

Marbled Chocolate Orange Olive Oil Cakes

Makes 12 mini Bundt cakes or one 9-inch loaf

These rich cakes are made with olive oil, almond flour and zingy orange zest. For a non-dairy version, replace the buttermilk with almond milk or coconut milk.

INGREDIENTS

3 large organic free-range eggs

1 cup organic cane sugar

¾ cup organic buttermilk, almond milk or coconut milk

¾ cup olive oil, plus more for greasing

Grated zest from 2 organic oranges

1½ cups organic spelt or whole-wheat flour

2 teaspoons organic baking powder

½ teaspoon salt

½ cup organic almond flour

4 ounces organic dark chocolate, coarsely chopped

DIRECTIONS

1. Preheat the oven to 350°F and generously grease 12 mini Bundt pans.

2. In the bowl of a mixer, combine the eggs, sugar, buttermilk, olive oil and orange zest.

3. In a large bowl, sift together the flour and baking powder. Mix in the salt and almond flour until combined.

4. Add the flour mixture to the egg mixture, mixing just until blended.

5. Using a microwave or double boiler, melt the chocolate. Transfer ⅓ of the batter to a bowl and then mix in the melted chocolate until smooth.

6. Pour some of the white batter into each of the pans and then pour in some chocolate batter. Draw a knife through the batter to make a marbled effect and then transfer to the oven.

7. Bake for about 40 minutes, or until a toothpick inserted in the middle of the cake comes out dry with crumbs. Cool the cakes in their pans for about 15 minutes and then invert onto a wire rack to cool completely.

8. May be stored in an airtight container for up to 3 days.

Makes 7 small muffins

See photo page 124

A healthier way of incorporating sweets in your diet can often be achieved by simply reducing the size of the treat. For example, by making muffins in a cupcake pan rather than a muffin pan, you'll make individual servings smaller right from the start. These, which incorporate both fresh apples and applesauce, have excellent texture and flavor.

INGREDIENTS

1 large organic free-range egg, room temperature

¼ cup organic unsweetened applesauce

½ cup organic coconut oil or canola oil

6 tablespoons organic brown cane sugar

2 organic apples, peeled and cored

1 cup organic spelt or whole-wheat flour

½ cup gluten-free organic oat flour

1 teaspoon baking soda

1½ teaspoons organic baking powder

Pinch of salt

½ teaspoon organic ground cinnamon

Pinch of ground organic nutmeg

½ cup chopped organic walnuts

½ cup organic light raisins, soaked overnight in water

1 tablespoon finely chopped organic crystallized ginger

DIRECTIONS

1. Preheat the oven to 350°F and line a cupcake pan with paper liners.

2. In a large mixing bowl, combine the egg, applesauce, oil and brown sugar. Grate one of the apples and mix in until combined.

3. In a separate bowl, sift together the flours, baking soda, baking powder, salt, cinnamon and nutmeg.

4. Add the flour mixture to the apple mixture, mixing just until combined. Cut the remaining apple into cubes and fold into the mixture, along with the walnuts, raisins and ginger.

5. Fill the paper liners until they are three-quarters full and bake for about 20 minutes, until the muffins are stable and a toothpick inserted in the center comes out dry. Transfer the cupcakes to a wire rack and let them cool to room temperature.

6. May be stored in an airtight container stored for up to 3 days.

Makes 20 small muffins

Here's a light recipe for enjoying summer zucchini. It's a healthier twist on ordinary zucchini muffins, as it replaces some of the oil with applesauce, uses spelt flour instead of ordinary flour and incorporates more vegetables. We've used a cupcake pan to make these muffins a bit smaller than ordinary muffins. If you use a muffin pan, you'll make about 16 muffins.

INGREDIENTS

1 cup organic cane sugar

½ cup organic coconut oil or canola oil

½ cup organic unsweetened applesauce

2 large organic free-range eggs, room temperature

½ cup organic buttermilk

1½ teaspoons organic pure vanilla extract

2 cups organic spelt or whole-wheat flour

½ cup gluten-free organic oat flour

¼ cup organic cocoa powder

1 teaspoon organic baking soda

½ teaspoon organic baking powder

¼ teaspoon salt

2 cups grated organic zucchini

1 cup organic chocolate chips or chopped organic dark chocolate

DIRECTIONS

1. Preheat the oven to 350°F and line a cupcake pan with paper liners.

2. In a large mixing bowl, combine the sugar, oil, applesauce, eggs, buttermilk and vanilla extract.

3. In a separate bowl, sift together the flours, cocoa, baking soda, baking powder and salt. Add the flour mixture to the wet mixture, mixing just until combined.

4. Fold in the zucchini and the chocolate chips, mixing just until combined. Make sure you don't overmix.

5. Fill the paper liners until they are three-quarters full and bake for about 15 minutes until the muffins are stable, and a toothpick inserted in the center comes out dry. Transfer the cupcakes to a wire rack and let them cool to room temperature.

6. May be stored in an airtight container for up to 3 days.

Makes 24 cupcakes

INGREDIENTS

Carrot Cupcakes

1 cup organic brown cane sugar

½ cup organic coconut oil or canola oil

¼ cup organic unsweetened applesauce

2 large organic free-range eggs, room temperature

1 cup organic spelt or whole-wheat flour

⅓ cup organic quinoa flour

¼ cup baking soda

1 teaspoon organic ground cinnamon

½ teaspoon organic ground ginger

⅛ teaspoon organic ground nutmeg

2 cups (⅔ pound) grated organic carrots

½ cup chopped organic walnuts

¼ cup organic light raisins, soaked in tea to soften

¼ cup organic shredded coconut

2 teaspoons finely chopped crystallized ginger

Cream Cheese Frosting

9 ounces organic cream cheese

6 tablespoons organic butter

1 cup organic cane confectioners' sugar

1 teaspoon organic ground ginger

Organic crystallized ginger, for garnish

In this refreshing alternative to traditional carrot cupcakes, nutty spelt and quinoa flour are used instead of white flour, and applesauce replaces some of the oil. Ginger adds a bit of sweet zing to the batter. Serve without frosting (see photo) for a lovely mid-morning snack or top with the cheesy frosting described below.

DIRECTIONS

1. Prepare the cupcakes: Preheat the oven to 350°F and line a cupcake pan with paper liners.

2. In a large mixing bowl, combine the sugar, oil and applesauce for about 1 minute until smooth. Add the eggs one at a time, mixing well after each addition.

3. In a separate bowl, sift together the flours, baking soda, cinnamon, ginger and nutmeg. Add the flour mixture to the wet mixture, mixing just until combined.

4. Fold in the carrots, walnuts, raisins, coconut and ginger, mixing just until combined. Make sure you don't overmix.

5. Fill the paper liners until they are three-quarters full and bake for 15 to 20 minutes, until the tops are puffed up and stable, and a toothpick inserted in the center comes out dry. Transfer the cupcakes to a wire rack and let them cool to room temperature. At this stage, the cupcakes may be stored in an airtight container for up to 3 days.

6. Prepare the frosting: In the bowl of an electric mixer, combine the cream cheese and butter until light and smooth. Beat in the confectioners' sugar and ground ginger until smooth.

7. Just before serving, top the cupcakes with frosting, garnish with ginger and serve. Frosted cupcakes may be stored in an airtight container in the refrigerator for up to 2 days.

Chocolate Hazelnut Mini Cupcakes

Makes 20 cupcakes

These cupcakes have no flour, but they do have a bit of corn starch. We find they taste best when made with dairy cream, but you can certainly make them with coconut cream and replace the butter with coconut oil or canola oil to make a delicious non-dairy version. The frosting is also vegan—it's made with just chocolate and coconut cream. Make sure you prepare the frosting one night in advance so it can chill thoroughly before whipping.

INGREDIENTS

Chocolate Hazelnut Cupcakes

9 ounces organic dark chocolate, coarsely chopped

½ cup organic cane sugar

2½ ounces organic butter, coconut oil or canola oil

½ cup organic dairy cream or coconut cream

2½ ounces gluten-free corn starch

3 large organic free-range eggs, room temperature

½ cup coarsely chopped organic hazelnuts

Chocolate Frosting

9 ounces organic dark chocolate, coarsely chopped

1 cup organic coconut cream

DIRECTIONS

1. Prepare the cupcakes: Preheat the oven to 350°F and line a mini cupcake pan with paper liners.

2. Place the chocolate, sugar, butter and cream in a double boiler and heat over medium heat until smooth and evenly combined. Cool to room temperature.

3. Mix in the corn starch until texture is smooth. Add the eggs, one at a time, mixing thoroughly after each addition.

4. Fold in the hazelnuts until combined.

5. Spoon the batter into the cupcake liners until three-quarters full and bake for about 15 minutes or until a toothpick inserted in the center comes out dry. Transfer to a wire rack and cool to room temperature. At this stage, the cupcakes may be stored in an airtight container for up to 3 days.

6. Prepare the frosting: Place the chocolate in a heatproof bowl. In a small pot, heat the coconut cream until it almost boils. Pour the coconut cream onto the chocolate and mix until smooth. Let the mixture cool to room temperature and then transfer to the refrigerator to cool overnight.

7. Just before serving, transfer the chilled chocolate mixture to a large mixing bowl and whip until light and airy. Transfer to a pastry bag and pipe onto the cupcakes. Frosted cupcakes may be stored in an airtight container in the refrigerator for up to 2 days.

Makes 18 squares

INGREDIENTS

Syrup

1½ cups organic cane sugar

1¼ cups water

2 tablespoons organic honey, date honey, maple syrup or agave syrup

1 organic cinnamon stick or vanilla pod, a few organic cardamom pods, or a dash of organic flavoring (such as rose water or orange blossom)

Semolina Cake

4 large organic free-range eggs, room temperature

⅔ cup organic coconut oil, canola oil, pumpkin oil or grape seed oil

¾ cup + 1 tablespoon freshly squeezed organic orange juice

Grated zest from 1 organic orange

½ cup organic brown cane sugar

⅔ cup organic almond flour

¾ cup organic whole-wheat or buckwheat flour

1 cup organic whole-wheat semolina

3 teaspoons organic baking powder

Coconut Chantilly (page 23), for serving

Organic pomegranate seeds, for serving

These squares have a marvelous texture and juicy spiced syrup. For a really moist cake, make sure there is a difference between the temperature of the cake and that of the syrup. For this reason, prepare the syrup well in advance to allow it to cool and pour it over the warm cake as soon as it comes out of the oven. We've served it here with Chantilly Cream, but you can also serve with fresh fruit or top with tahini and date honey.

DIRECTIONS

1. Prepare the syrup: In a small pot, combine the sugar, water and honey. If you are adding a whole spice, such as a cinnamon stick, add it here too. Bring the mixture to a boil over medium-high heat and cook for 3 to 5 minutes, until a syrup forms.

2. Pour the syrup through a fine mesh strainer. If you are adding a flavor extract, mix it in now. Set aside to cool while you prepare the cake.

3. Prepare the cake: Preheat the oven to 350°F and line a 9-inch square baking pan with parchment paper.

4. In a mixing bowl, combine the eggs, oil, orange juice and orange zest.

5. In a separate bowl, combine the sugar, flours, semolina and baking powder. Mix until thoroughly combined.

6. Add the dry ingredients to the wet ingredients and stir just until combined. Transfer to the baking pan and bake for about 25 minutes, until the top of the cake is golden and a toothpick inserted in the center comes out dry.

7. Remove the cake from the oven and immediately pour the cooled syrup on top, gradually and evenly. Set the cake aside to cool and absorb the syrup.

8. May be stored in an airtight container for up to 3 days. Serve with Coconut Chantilly and top with fresh pomegranate seeds.

Orange Almond Cake

Makes one 8-inch round cake

This flour-free cake contains almond flour rather than wheat flour, oil rather than butter, and an elegant touch of orange zest. For an additional flavor dimension, use coconut oil instead of butter and add ½ cup of shredded coconut. Easy to prepare and no need to divide the eggs.

INGREDIENTS

3 large organic free-range eggs, room temperature

¾ cup organic cane sugar

⅓ cup freshly squeezed organic orange juice

Grated zest from 1 organic orange

⅓ cup organic coconut oil, canola oil or grape seed oil

3 cups organic almond flour

DIRECTIONS

1. Preheat the oven to 350°F and oil an 8-inch round cake pan.

2. In the bowl of an electric mixer, beat the eggs and sugar for 5 to 7 minutes until the mixture is light, airy and creamy.

3. Gently fold in the orange juice, orange zest, oil and almond flour, folding until evenly combined.

4. Pour the batter into the pan and bake for 45 minutes, or until the top of the cake is stable and a toothpick inserted into the middle comes out dry with moist crumbs. Transfer to a wire rack and cool for 10 minutes before serving.

5. May be stored in an airtight container for up to 3 days.

Date and Honey Gugelhupf

Makes 1 Bundt cake

This vegan dessert is a classic Bundt cake flavored with date honey and warm spices, including cinnamon, ginger and cloves. If you like, replace the date honey with maple syrup or regular honey.

INGREDIENTS

2 cups organic spelt or whole-wheat flour

1 cup organic almond flour

¾ cup organic brown cane sugar

3 teaspoons organic baking powder

1 teaspoon organic ground cinnamon

½ teaspoon organic ground ginger

¼ teaspoon organic ground cloves

1½ cups organic unsweetened applesauce

¾ cup organic canola oil, vegetable oil or grape seed oil, plus more for greasing

¾ cup organic date honey, maple syrup or honey

DIRECTIONS

1. Preheat the oven to 350°F and generously grease a Bundt cake pan.

2. In a large mixing bowl, combine the flours, brown sugar, baking powder, cinnamon, ginger and cloves.

3. In a separate bowl, combine the applesauce, oil and date honey.

4. Combine the dry and wet ingredients until thoroughly mixed, and then transfer to the Bundt pan. Bake for 30 to 35 minutes until the cake is golden, and a toothpick inserted in the center comes out dry with moist crumbs.

5. Cool in the pan for about 15 minutes and then invert the cake onto a rack and cool completely before serving.

6. May be stored in an airtight container for up to 3 days.

Pumpkin Pecan Cake

Makes one Bundt cake

When autumn is in the air, this cake is perfect for greeting it. Fragrant and heartwarming, it will surely warm your heart (and stomach)!

INGREDIENTS

2 cups organic spelt or whole-wheat flour

2 tablespoons organic baking powder

1 teaspoon organic baking soda

2 teaspoons organic pumpkin pie spice

¼ teaspoon salt

3 large organic free-range eggs, room temperature

¾ cup organic date honey, honey or maple syrup

½ cup organic coconut oil or canola oil

½ cup organic buttermilk

2 tablespoons bourbon whiskey, optional

12 ounces organic pumpkin puree

½ cup coarsely chopped raw organic pecans

Organic cane confectioners' sugar, for sprinkling

DIRECTIONS

1. Preheat the oven to 350°F and grease a Bundt cake pan.

2. In a large bowl, sift together the flour, baking powder and baking soda.

3. In the bowl of an electric mixer, combine the pumpkin pie spice, salt, eggs, date honey, oil, buttermilk and bourbon. Mix until thoroughly combined.

4. Add the flour mixture to the egg mixture, mixing just until combined.

5. Fold in the pumpkin puree and pecans until evenly combined. Take care not to overmix.

6. Spoon the batter into the Bundt pan and bake for about 45 minutes, or until a toothpick inserted in the middle of the cake comes out with crumbs.

7. Cool in the pan for about 15 minutes and then invert the cake onto a rack to cool completely.

8. When cake is completely cooled, sprinkle with confectioners' sugar.

9. May be stored in an airtight container for up to 3 days

Chocolate Pecan Cake

Makes one 8-inch round cake

This cake contains avocado oil—a vegan oil with a slightly nutty flavor that has antioxidants, omegas and no cholesterol. It's also flour-free.

INGREDIENTS

Chocolate Pecan Cake

1 cup raw organic pecans

6 ounces organic dark chocolate, coarsely chopped

6 ounces organic avocado oil, coconut oil or melted organic butter

4 large organic free-range eggs, separated

½ cup + ¼ cup organic cane sugar

¼ teaspoon salt

Chocolate Frosting

5½ ounces organic dark chocolate, coarsely chopped

¾ cup coconut milk

DIRECTIONS

1. Prepare the cake: Preheat the oven to 325°F. Grease an 8-inch round cake pan and line with parchment paper.

2. Place the pecans on a baking sheet and toast for about 10 minutes until brown and fragrant. Cool to room temperature and then transfer to a food processor and process until ground.

3. Using a microwave or double boiler, heat the chocolate until melted. Mix in the oil until smooth.

4. In the bowl of a mixer, combine the egg whites with ½ cup of the sugar. Whisk until a stable foam forms, and then transfer to a clean bowl and set aside.

5. Place the egg yolks in the bowl of the mixer and add the remaining ¼ cup of sugar and salt. Beat until a light cream forms.

6. Add the chocolate mixture to the egg yolk mixture and blend until a smooth cream forms. Fold in the ground pecans until evenly mixed.

7. Using a rubber spatula, gradually fold in the whisked egg whites until combined. Transfer the batter to the cake pan and bake for 35 minutes, or until a toothpick inserted in the center comes out dry with moist crumbs. Transfer to a wire rack and cool to room temperature. If you want the top of the cake to be smooth, turn the cake over after about 15 minutes and let it cool upside-down on the rack.

8. Prepare the frosting: Using a double boiler or microwave, melt the chocolate. In a small pot, heat the coconut milk until it almost boils. Pour the coconut milk into the melted chocolate and mix until smooth.

9. Pour the frosting on the cake, smoothing it on the top and sides with a spatula. Transfer to the refrigerator and chill until frosting hardens. Serve at room temperature.

10. May be stored in the refrigerator in an airtight container for up to 3 days.